Beyond the east wind

LEGENDS AND FOLKTALES OF VIETNAM

Told by
DUONG VAN QUYEN

Written by
JEWELL REINHART COBURN

Illustrated by
NENA GRIGORIAN ULLBERG

By Jewell Reinhart Coburn

BEYOND THE EAST WIND:
Legends and Folktales of Vietnam

KHMERS, TIGERS AND TALISMANS:
From the History and Legends of
Mysterious Cambodia

ENCIRCLED KINGDOM:
Legends and Folktales of Laos

SECOND PRINTING, 1981

Text copyright © 1976 Jewell Reinhart Coburn and Duong, Van Quyen
Illustrations copyright © 1976 Nena Grigorian Ullberg and Jewell Reinhart Coburn

Burn, Hart and Company Publishers
Thousand Oaks ● Box 1772 ● California 91360

Duong, Van Quyen and Coburn, Jewell Reinhart, Beyond the East Wind, Legends and Folktales of Vietnam.
SUMMARY: ten tales: Lac Long Quan and Au Co, The Legend of the Betel, Hung Vuong and the Earth and Sky Cakes, Lizards and Promises and Vue Cong Due, Monsoon, Crystal Love, Turtles of Gold and Bitter Regrets, A Strange and Rare Friendship, The Sister Queens, The Lady of Nam Xuong. [1. Folklore 2. Vietnam] Ullberg, Nena Grigorian, ill.
II. Title. 76-50345
ISBN 0-918060-01-X

Printed in the United States of America

DEDICATION

When we turned from our land, left behind us the laughter of our loved ones, the familiarity of our way of life, we came away with empty hands and very heavy hearts.

Because of your compassion and generosity our hands and minds are full. We smile with lifted spirits.

But how can we say thank you? In what way can we express our appreciation?

Not able to turn outward, we have instead turned inward. . .to that which knows no marked value, no tags of cost or duty. . .but rather to that which is beyond price. . .that which is to us most precious.

Thus is this book — a collection of our country's best loved tales retold and illustrated with care to authenticity of theme, mood, and detail.— a gift from our culture to your culture. . . from our hearts to your hearts.

We dedicate this book to you, our American friends.

CONTENTS

NOTES

THE
LEGENDARY ORIGIN
OF
THE COUNTRY
OF
VIETNAM

LAC LONG QUAN AND AU CO

In that far away time - long before men and women peopled the world - it is said that a great mist enveloped the earth. It rolled and swirled and heaved, and embraced in a majestic silver hue all that was.

Mountains reached skyward in a graceful sweep then spread wide into endless misted meadows. Stones lay sculped, molded and solid. Streams flowed in measured movement. There were no thorns. No strangling vines, no menacing roots. No poisonous blooms with sword-sharp leaves - only a peaceful, pervasive, serene perfection.

until...

out from the mighty sea, from the midst of a thunderous surf, out of the raging foam, burst a being who when he stood full height on his wave-lashed shore stood taller than the highest mountain, more solid than the densest rock, fiercer than the most raging monsoon. His scaled body was as layers of the finest bronze. His eyes piercing, as sharp, flashing swords. Long and sharp

7

were his mighty claws - powerful, his great, strong tail.

Lac Long Quan was the mighty Dragon, ruler of the sea. And when he came from the waters, he came with dignity, with purpose, and with plan.

Now at the same time there lived in the remotest reaches of the farthest mountains a creature of unequaled beauty. Her form was lithesome and graceful and wherever she walked the wind sang and the leaves brushed in rhythmic counterpoint. When she spoke the air about her became lyrical and exquisite melody swirled among the trees and pale petaled blossoms. Her name was Au Co, the fairy queen of the mountains, and she ruled the land with a gentle hand.

And so it was that in that instant, that interval in time when the king of the seas first gazed upon the queen of the mountains that the mighty waves of the great waters stilled and the sea stood mirrored in silver silence. The mountain mists ceased their rolling. They hung motionless - their gray, an iridescent calm. There was no movement. No sound. Time lay hushed and mute.

In that instant the great Lac Long Quan and the beautiful Au Co seemed to recognize that they had always been meant to venture from their distant realms to meet one another in this misted dawn of earliest time.

"Never have I known such beauty as is yours, Fair Queen of the Mountains," murmured the giant dragon of the Sea. "Such delicacy is not to be found in my kingdom at the green-black depths of the oceans."

And the great ruler of the water, mighty in every other way, stood in speechless awe before so gentle a creature as the lovely Au Co.

In demure silence, Au Co found herself equally spellbound. "Such strength and power... such immensity," she thought. And she sensed what it might be to be protected and directed by such might.

So the king of the Sea reached forth toward the Fairy Queen of the Mountains and she extended her fragile hand in return. Their love drew together the waters of the seas and the lands of the earth. Their love united power and beauty.

As the days and nights of time took form and as the waters and lands grew more distinct, each with its own gift to the whole of creation, so it was that the moment came when the seas roared in triumph and the winds sang with happiness for it was learned that the Dragon's fair queen was to give royal birth.

The mighty king dived and plunged and paced in anticipation, his great tail lashing valleys and inlets in the soft earth's surface. The surface clapped in celebration against the sandy shoulders of the ocean's shores. And the waves stood high in salute then sang with joy as they rolled back into the sea.

Then, just as the formless past yields to the form of future...a tumultuous shout! And there, revealed in magnificience, not one, not two, nor even fifty, but one hundred perfect and beautiful sons sprung from one hundred perfect pearl-shelled eggs.

9

Happiness shone like a dazzling sun. It dissolved the haze and exposed a new day, crystaline and brilliant.

And so it was that the great Dragon and the Fairy Queen nurtured their one hundred sons until the day it was revealed that they had grown strong and ready to rule themselves.

The great Dragon then called for his queen and he explained to her how two so very different as a dragon and a fairy could not be expected to live together forever but must at some point in time return to their origin.

"So be it, my King," said the dutiful fairy queen and she took fifty of their sons and they returned to the mountains. These sons became the mountain and hill tribes of Vietnam known for their skills in hunting and upland farming.

The great Dragon took the other fifty sons to the sea and they became Vietnam's renowned fishermen and lowland farmers.

And then Lac Long Quan called the first born of the one hundred sons to himself and was pleased to see that he had grown into fine manhood. He gave to him the title of Hung Vuong and he became the founder of the very first, the mighty Hung Vuong dynasty that lasted from 2879 to 258 B.C.[1]

To this very day the tenth day of the third month of the lunar calendar[2] is a time set aside for all Vietnamese to reflect on their country's very earliest beginning.

THE LEGEND OF THE BETEL

Long ago in the far northern kingdom of Vietnam there lived two almost perfectly identical twin brothers. These brothers were so alike that villagers thought of them as two perfect drops of rain - perfectly alike in their young handsomeness and perfectly alike in the love they bore for each other. It was as though they had fallen, together, fully formed from heaven.

One day, their mother watched them as they made their ways along the dikes separating the rice paddies that lay shimmering in the late afternoon sun.

She saw that the boys had grown strong and tanned and that Cao Tan, the slightly older twin, took his place in the lead, the heavy plow over his shoulder. Cao Lang, the barely younger twin, followed devotedly, leading the great buffalo that helped them in their fields.

It was time, she thought, to find a wife for Cao Tan.

Now there was in a nearby village a very lovely girl named Xuan Phu who the twins' mother knew she could love as a daughter. The girl was as fair as a soft breeze yet as sturdy as young bamboo.

The twin's widowed mother sought the hand of the lovely girl. Her parents, thinking as highly of the fine sons as did the rest of the villagers, were pleased with the arrangement. They were satisfied knowing their daughter would become a member of an honored family.

Yet, unknown to anyone, not only did Cao Tan love the beautiful Xuan Phu but Cao Lang had also seen her and fallen in love with her. But Cao Lang dared not reveal his feelings because of his deep respect for his mother and his love for his older twin brother.

Plans were laid for the wedding. Laughter and excitement danced in the air and the day finally arrived when Cao Tan brought his bride to his home. No one guessed how the younger twin's heart nearly broke within him.

Many suns set and one day Cao Tan stayed in the field later than usual so it was the younger twin who lifted the plow to his shoulder and walked on home first.

13

The young wife, seeing what she thought to be her husband making his way along the dikes carrying the plow, laid down her embroidery and flung aside the cares of the day and went out into the languid afternoon sun to meet him.

Cao Lang saw her as she came toward him. He set down his burden and watched her. She approached him and placed her hand tenderly on his arm.

Just then Xuan Phu realized her mistake but by that time Cao Tan had come upon them and he, not realizing the error that had taken place, allowed his face to show his displeasure. Sad days passed and ill feeling blew like a chill autumn wind over the once love-filled little house.

Cao Lang grieved that he had appeared to wrong his older brother and felt ashamed of his love for the young wife. It was not his wish to bring sorrow or dishonor to his family yet his heart would give him no peace.

In the deep black of one night he stole away so as to cause no further family sadness. He wandered away from the house, beyond the rice fields and along the paths that he knew so well. He walked through the tall grass and on and on until nothing any longer was familiar to him. He groped and stumbled his way until he knew that he was in the far forbidden jungles.

The air was heavy and breathless. Branches entwined him. Vines encircled him. Fallen trees covered the paths and thick leaves hid his way.

Day after day he struggled on and day after day he grew more and more weary. Finally he knew himself to be hopelessly lost. He sank to the jungle floor, fevered and ill.

He looked about him and for the first time saw the strange beauty of the place where he lay. The fierce jungle seemed to stand back as if respectful of so beautiful a spot. In the clearing, the grass grew like rich velvet and a stream flowed like ribbons of crystal.

Never had Cao Lang seen such a sight. Farther and farther away drifted his dreams of the straight, predictable paths of the familiar rice fields, and the little house he knew he must leave. Farther and farther wafted the image of the beautiful girl for whom he bore such love yet knew he could never have. He was left only with the iron-like bond that would not loose him from the memory of his brother who was so much a part of him.

There, he died and after a time there appeared where he lay a stone of strange beauty - feather soft and purest white.

At home the elder brother repented his anger and longed for his younger brother who was so like him that at times they shared a single crystal thought.

Days dawned and waned and Cao Tan knew he could not be complete nor could he ever again know happiness without Cao Lang. Filled with regret and sorrow, he set out to search for his brother and to bring him home.

Cao Tan's journey took him over great mountains and steep precipices, up wide rivers and through terrible currents until finally he too became hopelessly lost in the far jungles.

After many days of futile wandering and climbing, Cao Tan stumbled, hungry and also fevered, upon the very clearing where his brother had fallen into his final sleep. There he saw the rich carpet of velvet green. He too saw the crystal stream that flowed nearby. And there, in the middle of the clearing, he saw the exquisite stone - as pure white as the underside of a young dove's wing. In his grief, he too sank to the ground, lay back against the beautiful stone and there too, he died.

When her young husband did not return, the lovely wife felt she must set about to find him. So she bid her loving mother-in-law good-bye and ran toward the mountains like an iridescent sun beam races an early shining dawn.

Some wistful feeling guided her way along the rice fields, through the tall grasses and into the thick mountain forests. Heavy jungle leaves seemed to part gently before her and the sun always stayed ahead of her to light her way. She walked on, tired but resolute, and after many days she came to a strange clearing. There, a shaft of sun penetrated the dark undergrowth and in the very center, set majestically apart, stood the most magnificent tree she had ever seen.

It rose strong and straight, high above all the other trees and at its very top great graceful fronds waved in a halo of jungle sun. At its base was the exquisite stone of dove white.

The young wife knew that this was no ordinary stone nor was the tree to which she was drawn by its unusual strength and beauty. The majesty of the tree spoke to her of the respect with which she had honored her young husband. The mystery of its attraction spoke to her of the inexplainable love they had known.

She had no wish to return to her lonely hut near the rice fields. Her only desire was to sit near the stone and look high into the leaves of the tree.

Years passed and one day the great king, Hung Vuong, was hunting in the jungle. He came upon a magnificent sight and called to his huntsmen who crowded about him.

They all gazed up into the great tree whose bare trunk was curiously entwined by a broad-leafed vine. They moved closer and saw that the vine seemed to be lovingly embracing the great tree. When the wind stirred ever so slightly, the leaves appeared to caress the mighty palm. At the base of the tree lay a stone of purest white.

"I am puzzled by such beauty. What does this mean?" inquired the king.

So his huntsmen, who from childhood had been told the legends of their land, unfolded to him the story of the three fatal loves.

The king was deeply touched by the story and he gazed long at the regal palm and the delicate vine that entwinted it. Finally the king said, "if these were such devoted brothers and if the husband and wife were so faithful, then let us unite the three and see the result."

So the king ordered his men to pick one of the nuts from the tree and one of the leaves from the plant. He placed them in his hand. Then he closed his palm over them. As he gently squeezed together the nut and the leaf a juice flowed out. Some of it fell on the white stone and there appeared drops of red - red as love itself.

The king was astonished and he declared, "This is indeed the true symbol of loyalty and love between brothers and between lovers."

So profoundly did this story speak to the king that upon leaving the jungle the great Hung Vuong issued the order that the tree and the plant be grown everywhere in commemoration of this tragic but beautiful tale. And he ordered his people to chew the three substances - symbolic of deep mutual affection.

From that time so long ago until this very day, the Betel nut, the leaf of the Betel Pepper, and a pellet of lime[3]- three symbols of a love that could not be destroyed - are used in all marriage ceremonies in Vietnam.

HUNG VUONG AND THE EARTH AND SKY CAKES

The contest could in no way be called ordinary. As a matter of record, nothing the great Hung Vuong did could be called ordinary. His lands stretched farther than any neighboring kingdoms. His wealth was grander. His armies mightier. Even his wives numbered more than the neighboring monarchs could boast. And his sons, well, as you might suppose, the great Hung Vuong had in his employ specially appointed scribes who did nothing but keep scrolls with current listings of each royal male birth. Each was categorized by name, birthdate, location, and identification number should the great king call for, as he now and then did, a periodic family up-date.

It is also a fact that the great Hung Vuong himself was no mere Vuong for were he the first of the Hung dynasty he would indeed have his firstness to boast. Or were he Hung Vuong the fifth or even the tenth, he would have at minimum his fifthness or tenthness to set him apart. But His Majesty was instead, none other than the peak of the line, the pick of the clan, the veritable dome of the dynasty, the extraordinary Hung Vuong the Seventeenth.

Thus was it fitting that he who was to follow be no mere number eighteen. No indeed, For one worthy to follow in so great a line must, of course, be unique. Hung would personally see to that.

So it was that the word filtered from the great chamber that Hung Vuong 17 was up to his trickiest, his cleverest, as a matter of fact that which would probably prove the crest of his career - his ultimate royal coup. His plan was near readiness and by that plan would his successor be chosen.

Thus did the many sons gather from every corner of the royal compound. They came with robust dreams of splendor and staunch lust for power. Hallways and courtyards became a hub-bub of speculation. They jostled one another with swordlike words with sharp double edges. Plots and counterplots were hatched and pecked at like hungry bantams in newly strewn grain.

Now each of the king's wives, wanting her son to be the chosen one, was keen for information. Bribes stirred the air like a capricious breeze playing about the corridors and alcoves of the royal residence.

Aunts, uncles, daughters, even first, second, and third cousins got in on the scene by playing out the roles of willing pawns and cooperative informants. How remarkably helpful did they suddenly become when tantalized by prospects of silver coins or places of esteem in return for those ever-so-small deeds well done.

"Self speaks for self," shrugged Hung's eldest and thus first born son. "No need for me to do anything other than I've always done, after all what more could such as I do anyway," he asked himself as he strutted arrogantly among the younger princes and mused to himself, "No matter what the contest, I, as the eldest son, will win merely by being who I am." And he went about his dallying ways confident that he would soon enjoy a monarch's stamp on his insufferable ways.

Son number 37 swaggered about among the other brothers flexing his great muscles. His physical prowess was known throughout the kingdom. There was not a feat of strength that Number 37 did not win and thus bring honor to the royal household. Well, except for that single rather insignificant event where at the crucial moment in the season's royal wrestling exhibitions, just as he was hoping to break the opponent's hold, he tripped somewhat ingloriously over his sandal string and sprawled comically on the mat. But that would be stricken from the royal records - naturally. As would all snickers be ordered silenced - of course. Thus, whatever be the contest, Number 37 was assured of his place because no man could boast of this son's strength, physical endurance, or influence over royal record keepers.

Now son number 92 was not a mingler. He kept his distance from the other less gifted princes. He pulled his scholar's robes about him, thrust his nose high in the air and sat alone and always slightly above the others. His was to contemplate the implicit faith he held in the strength of his intellect which, he thought, would equip him whatever the test.

At just that moment, for the great Hung Vuong 17 chose his moments with exquisite care, the great doors to the royal chamber moved. All attention turned in their direction. They opened slowly...but only slightly.

"By all the spirits around us, what is this?" growled the strongest son quietly under his breath so no one could accuse him of disrespect. "Is this why we have been called together?" And he fisted his great hands and pretended to spar with the air.

"Such an indignity," thought the scholar son. And he wrapped his robes yet closer about him and thrust his nose yet higher in the air.

"Such an important message to be given in so clever a way!" came a clear, young voice from within the milling crowd of restless sons. "Only a great father could think of such a scheme."

Instead of the king appearing, as was expected, the two great guards at the chamber doors leaned down and lifted like a Longan leaf the youngest, the very shiest of all His Majesty's small messenger boys.

The guards placed him on one of the highest steps where he was able to look out over the great hoard of surly princes.

The small boy timidly raised the large scroll before him - the great seal of Hung Vuong 17 clearly visible to all.

In the meekest, tiniest of voices, the little boy commanded the attention of all those older and grander than himself.

Thus did he read:

> As the New Year is a time when the children of
> the land pay tribute to their parents with feasting and
> gifts, so it will be this New Year when each of the royal
> sons will present to his father a tribute in the form of a
> delicious and unusual meal of his own making.

> Each dish is to be so thoughtfully prepared that
> it will not only fulfill the filial tradition but will also fulfill
> a final, most important requirement.

The hoard of sons stood tense and motionless like a riverbank thick with dry bamboo on a hot and windless afternoon.

> Only will he be worthy to please a father and
> rule a people who can prepare and present a dish that
> reveals his understanding of the mystery of life.

"So that is the plan, is it? Clever father I have," thought the eldest son. "For my part this will be simple. What my Queen mother does not know about foods and fathers isn't worth knowing."

21

"Ah so, grunted the strongest son as he thought to himself, "What I bring no man but the most powerful could produce. I'll show them all!" and he turned his lumbering body to leave only to find himself with both massive feet standing flatly on the hem of the scholar son's robes.

Everyone stopped and turned to watch this encounter for it was always an event of note to be a firsthand observer of conflict between royal brain and royal brawn.

With obvious distain, the scholar son looked into the eyes of his muscled brother and hissed under his breath, "If your meal is as elegant as you are graceful, I fear for my father's digestion." And with that he yanked his robe from under his brother's feet, hiked it up in both hands and was on his way, his nose, as always, high in the air.

A roar arose from the gathering. Laughter like young stallions pranced and bucked in the air. And each of the princes set out, confident that his would be the finest feast his father had ever tasted.

Soon, quiet returned to the royal courtyard. The compound seemed abandoned - all but for one young fellow left sitting near the great doors that led to the royal chamber. He sat motionless, a shabby, silent guitar at his side.

"A clever idea indeed," mused the boy, "to unravel the mystery of life by the common act of preparing a meal. But much too clever for me," he sighed and drew his guitar close to him and accompanied it with his quiet musings...

> I have no zeal for power,
>   nor am I inclined to rule.
> I have no hidden urges to
>   manipulate the fool,
> That I might by some cunning,
>   devise some artful plan

By which I might command
            the bent and broken man
Yet, if it somehow fell to me
            to have some humble say -
To have some opportunity
            to inspire my brothers
                on their way,
I think that it would likely be
            a somewhat simple prayer
That man renew respect for life
            and for that life to care.

And so the young man sat alone, sighing softly to the music of his friendly guitar. Night gathered and the young prince leaned back against the great doors. He had no desire to return to his lonely rooms at the farthest corner of the compound.

In time, he fell asleep and while he slept, there slipped quietly into his dream a rather curious sight. Standing squarely and comfortably within the lad's dream was what appeared to be an old man with a head of white and a beard of long, thin gray hair.

"You there, Young Man," the old man seemed to whisper. "You, sleeping by the chamber door." His voice was husky yet his appearance was kindly.

"Lad," he persisted.

The boy shifted his position slightly but didn't awaken.

"That's fine. You go ahead and sleep. I'll sit here beside you and lean against these doors too. No, you needn't stir, Lad. I'll talk to you while you rest. There's room for both of us and I can say what I have to say with you as you are."

The old man leaned back and nestled comfortably into the young man's dream. He went on, "Everyone expected to see the king himself today, didn't they? That is, everyone but you and I, of course. We both know that significances can be found in simplicities, don't we, Lad. And just as I know, you know that many things in life are other than they seem. Such is true of your great father also for why else would he have chosen this somewhat unusual manner to announce his plan for separating the wise princes from those less qualified?

"What sport to watch those arrogant fellows - full of their vain dreams - run scampering off in search of someone to do their work and to make their feast for them.

"You watch, Lad, the buying of recipes will become big business this season. The price of delicacies will soar and chefs will soon be among our land's wealthiest men. And rest assured, Lad, the great Hung Vuong 17 will note this too.

"But you, My Boy, will come to understand how foolish all this to be. No, you don't have to respond. Just lie there as you are. We can chat very well with you asleep. In fact, I tend to prefer it this way. Just between the two of us, I have a deuce of a time getting folks to see me when their eyes are open or to hear me even when they are listening.

"But you, Lad, well, I have been watching you for a very long time and I know you to have inherited much of the greatness of your remarkable father. Of course the king has a few royal peculiarities but then who of the best of us does not. Such as your own, shall we say, rather low estate within the royal family. But such is of no real consequence to us.

"As I was saying, while the others go about turning the heads and greasing the palms of every village cook, you and I will review some regal secrets and think some royal thoughts.

"Your great father decreed that only he who by the preparation of some artful dish which revealed his understanding of life could qualify to follow in the Great Line and bear the title of Hung Vuong 18. Now think on this, My Prince."

The old man gestured toward the sky. Suddenly, the clear, deep, star-strewn night gave way to the haze of dawn, then early morning and suddenly, although the lad slept on, it became full day - a blaze of brilliance.

And then the old man said:

Look about you, My Child, My Son.

Look to the sky, then the earth.

What do you see that speaks of a source -

of beginning,

becoming,

of birth?

Look high to the heaven.

Quite visibly, you'll see

In all His celestial majesty

burning full and round and hot

a force

which when He shines

on the earth

makes for

beginnings,

becomings,

and birth.

Then look to the Earth

who cradles Her young

Given Her by His Lordship, the Sun.

In turn She gives nurturing,

her own unique care,

that you and I

and mankind can share

her abundance.

So fashion your dream into two hearty cakes

that speak of the earth and the sky

For in so doing you've the secret of life,

and when you awake, you will know why

I entered your dream.

The boy awoke with a start. "How very strange," he puzzled. "I fell asleep with a sad heart and empty head and I awake full to overflowing. I seem to know exactly what to prepare for my father and exactly what each ingredient must be."

The young prince rubbed his eyes, and leaped to his feet.

The New Year season arrived with a burst of festivity. The air was static with excitement. Tables groaned with food of every description and sons stood by with faces unable to hide their pride.

Delicacy after delicacy was served to the great king. Each son explained the artistic combinations of herbs and seasonings contained in his own dish.

The days of feasting passed one by one until the very eve of the New Year. Only then was it the poor lad's turn to be summoned before the king.

"You Lad," the father waved him closer. "What have you prepared for this occasion? Step close, My Boy. When you hold back so I cannot see what you have."

The young prince stepped closer and knelt before his father, careful to keep his eyes lowered in respect.

"What? No corps of servants at your elbow? No ostentatious display?" quizzed the king. "Speak up, My Boy. What have you there?"

The young prince began, his head still low in deep respect, "Oh, Mighty Father and the most honored Hung Vuong in the Great Line of Hung rulers, I present to you my humble offering...these two small cakes."

"Yes, Yes, Boy," the king urged him on. "And what does each contain, Lad. What does each mean?"

And the young prince replied, "It came to me in a dream one night that the secret of life was not hidden, that it did not take any special key to open the door of life's mystery. But rather that all it really took were the tools each already has.

"What it does demand is a hearty look, the result of a questioning mind and, of course, a reverence for the quest as well as reverence for what we find."

"Go on, Boy. Go on," urged the king.

"So the first way I looked was up and of course the sun hung radiant and full. And I asked myself what would it be if that sun were to cease to shine. And the answer, of course, spoke of the source of life as we know it on earth."

"Yes, Yes, and then...?"

"So I took the leaf from the banana tree, and rice, so essential to life, and I steamed it and pounded it to a feathery white - piled it high in a powdery mound. Then I molded it round like the mighty sun and patted it firm and sound. And here before you, My Father, My King, the cake in the shape of the sun."

"Ah, hah," responded the king. "And then?"

"Second, I gathered more foods of the earth - dried peas, pork meat, and fine rice. These I prepared with special care and laid them on leaves layer by layer. It took on the shape of a square that was flat like the earth with its sun ripened fields.

"The foods of the people I shaped like their source. They tell of Earth Mother and Sun's life-giving force. Thus I present, Oh great Father and King, the substance life, the essence of fate, here on this platter, my Earth and Sky Cakes."

The mighty king looked upon this young lad who by his wisdom and by this deed stood out among the others. He put out his hand to him and as the lad lifted his face he found himself looking into a kindly regal face with a head of white and a beard of fine gray hair.

"By these two lowly cakes. You, My Son, have captured and placed before me in humble triumph your understanding of life. By these, you have caught life's meaning. The round cake, delicately made, represents the life-giving sun who when He shines on the earth helps Her produce food to sustain earthly life. And the square cake, made of the foods of the people, suggests by its shape the earth that produces these foods and on which the people dwell.

From this time forward, your gift will be a part of every New Year's celebration," continued his father. "Our people will follow your recipes and thus each year will they renew their respect for life. And as for you, My Boy, you will wear the crown and be known as Hung Vuong 18 because only wisdom such as yours is worthy of such a position."

And so it is that from that time until this, the round cake and the square cake are served at all Vietnamese New Year's gatherings. At all traditional Vietnamese weddings, it is the groom who brings the two cakes to his bride that she in turn might share them with the wedding guests.[4]

LIZARDS AND PROMISES
and
VU CONG DUE

If you watch at just the time the sun has slipped beyond the farthest mountain and the air it warmed hasn't yet given away to the chill of the night, you'll see him.

If you listen closely as the last of the cooking coals lose their glow and the wok is washed and hung away for frying tomorrow's rice, you'll hear him. That quick, clear "click-chuck" as though were he human he would be clicking his tongue against the roof of his mouth - like we do sometimes when we might like to say, "I could have told you that... if you'd merely asked me."

There he'd be up on the ceiling, hanging there, goodness knows how, and looking down as if wondering how it is that humans can be so un-reptile-like and thus so lacking in elemental wisdom.

I'm talking about Thạch Sùng, of course. The household lizard.

But I'm getting ahead of myself. I must begin at the beginning and that is with Vu Cong Due.[5]

Due was born in the country to a tenant farmer family. His parents were so wretchedly poor that both his father and his mother had to work at many jobs other than tending the crops for their landlord. This meant that young Due was often left in the shabby hut to do what he could to fill in for his absent parents.

Times were hard and they were growing steadily worse for Due's family. The landlord demanded more and more work yet less and less money jingled in his father's pockets.

While his parents were away, Due would go about the hut, whisking as clean as a young boy can whisk clean, the packed dirt floor of his hut. He brought water from the stream and kept a pot of it simmering so there would be boiled, clean water available at all times. He tended the few plants that provided the family with cabbage, and beets, and sweet potatoes.

When Due would finish his chores, he often wandered outside in search of old Trâu Khổng Lồ. Trâu[6] was the oldest, and at one time the most prized of the Lord's great water buffalo. He had pulled mighty loads of grain and had helped plow many a field in his day.

On his way, Due would select a specially tender bamboo shoot, tear off all of its leaves except for the few at the very end. When he found old Trâu, he would climb onto his powerful back, use the bamboo sprig to guide him, then lie back, and dream.

Now Due's dreams were, if all strung together like a chain of lichee nuts[7], really only a single dream. For when he gazed about him - over the vast green plains cut into small square rice paddies, beyond the pineapple fields and the longan[8] groves to the mountains rising nobly in the distant haze, he would lose himself - always in the same reverie.

"What lay beyond those mountains?" he wondered. "Were there villages larger than his own? Were there great numbers of people and did they look like him? Did they act like him? Were their lives at all like his? Did they know more than he knew?"

This last question bothered Due the most because he tended to feel that life beyond the mountains might somehow contain more answers than questions - that it might somehow hold more satisfactions than longings.

But no matter how Due's dreams could carry him to the very peaks of the distant mountains, he would always have to dream right back down their slopes, back across the fields, up the familiar path past the giant banyan tree and back to this very hut and hearth.

For it is this hut that was Due's and his parents' world, even though it and the land on which it sat belonged to someone else. Only those few meager utensils that had been in their family for years - handed down from mother to daughter or to son's wife - could this small family claim as their very own. There hung the gleaming wok - the pan in which many a ginger root and garlic clove had sizzled their fragrance into the small hut. There, the treasured tea pot - a fine crack timidly making its way along the ancient lid.

Now, although this hut and all that was around it was theirs to use so long as they pleased their landlord, still, the fact could not be overlooked that every man of integrity possessed a deep desire to own his own land no matter how small it might be. Due's father had approached the landlord about this but the landlord would always find some excuse to change the subject or otherwise discourage him.

Although Due never spoke of his own dreams to his parents, Due's mother and father had never successfully hidden their dream from him nor could they hide the difficult times they were having.

So it was that Due had overheard his parents speaking of their decision to borrow money from one of the village's richest men ... just enough to try to make ends meet and to keep their dream alive.

This was not easy for Due's parents to do for although they were poor, they were proud people who wanted to enjoy the benefits of their own labors. But for the time, there was no other choice but the one they made.

Even after they had received the loan Due's mother and father continued their diligent work. Yet somehow, the money seemed to dwindle.

The day finally arrived when the payment of the loan was due. Due's parents had left for their labors that morning with very heavy hearts. They were unable to repay their debt.

The Lender went to the poor farmer's hut. Dressed in the heavy black silk of a man who knows success in matters of money, he stood at the doorway sternly peering in.

"Where are your parents, Lad?" the man inquired. Due set his broom down in the corner of the kitchen and went to the door.

"They are not at home." replied the boy.

"Their payment is due and I must know their whereabouts," insisted the Lender.

"But they are working just now," the boy explained.

"Then tell me where they are working." persisted the man.

"If you must know exactly where they are," the boy replied, "I will tell you."

And so he said,

> My father has gone to kill the living plants and to plant the
>> dead ones.
> My mother has gone to sell the wind and to buy a forest.

The man studied the boy. At first he thought he had not heard him correctly so he asked him once more.

The boy obliged and repeated what he had said the first time:

> My father has gone to kill the living plants and to plant the
>> dead ones.
> My mother has gone to sell the wind and to buy a forest.

The man thought and thought. He paced back and forth in front of the hut. He rubbed his chin. He sat on the great protruding root of the ancient banyan tree, and he gazed at the sky. Still he was puzzled by what the boy said.

Finally he called to the boy and again Due stopped his work and approached the rich man.

"Son," he said, rising from the tree root and putting his hand on Due's shoulder. "Perhaps you could tell me one more time where your parents are."

34

So Due dutifully repeated what he had already said.

My father has gone to kill the living plants and to plant the
dead ones.
My mother has gone to sell the wind and to buy a forest.

This time the rich man stood up and he paced furiously. He clutched at his chin and sat down hard on the outcropped root. He stared intently at the ground.

Charged by impatience and curiosity, the rich man leaped up and caught the boy by the arm.

"Look here, Boy," he said. "You explain to me what you mean and I'll forget the debt your parents owe me."

At this prospect, the boy's heart leaped within him. But he dared not reveal his joy. He knew that the debt was not yet actually set aside. He must remain composed.

So the boy paused. He looked at the ground. He let his toe work a small hole in the soft earth. Then he looked up at the anxious man and said, "Kind Sir, I deeply appreciate your proposal. Because you are a good businessman, I know you'll gladly offer proof that you'll stand by your side of the bargain."

"Come now, my boy," the Lender urged. "I am a grown man and grown men don't betray young children."

But the boy stood firm. With great courtesy, Due requested that the wealthy man produce a witness.

Just then, the rich man looked through the doorway of the hut and into the kitchen. There, as he always appeared at just that time when the sun slips beyond the farthest mountain and the cooking coals lose their glow was Thach Sung.

Due could see him balanced on the tips of the great cooking chopsticks from which he always made his spring toward the ceiling. They were propped against the stove.

"There," the man pointed confidently. "There is our witness." Both glanced upward for Thach Sung by that instant was already looking down at them. To the rich man's suggestion Thach Sung seemed to give a most earnest "click-chuck."

Now while you and I might have our doubts as to the wisdom of such a choice, Due seemed to have a special insight. Don't forget, Thạch Sũng was like a member of the family and we know there can be special understandings among family folk.

So it was with no hesitation that Due agreed to the selection.

The Lender felt smug that he had so cunningly trapped this country lad.

So the boy leaned against the trunk of the ancient banyan tree that had for so many years given the only shade to the humble little shack and he gave this explanation:

> When my father goes out to kill the living plants
> he is pulling the tender young rice shoots out of their small
> fertile beds.

> When he is planting the dead plants, he is placing
> those shoots that could die if they were left exposed to the
> killing air into new growing beds so they'll have more
> nourishment and more room to grow larger and produce
> more grain.

> When I told you that my mother had gone to
> sell the wind, I was saying that my mother had gone to the
> market place to sell the fans she makes in her evening
> hours.

> When I said she had gone to buy the forest, I

was saying that with the money she makes from selling the

fans, she buys the necessary bamboo to make more.

With this explanation, the Lender's curiosity was satisfied. With the promise to forget the debt barely out of his lips, he went smiling on his way.

But the man had other ideas. He was going to have his money no matter what his promise had been. So within a few days he was again at Due's hut demanding payment.

This time he found the father and mother at home. But no matter how the family protested, the rich man countered with the accusation that the boy was full of lies and that the parents must stand by their agreement and repay their debt.

It did indeed begin to appear that the clever businessman would win his cause for he was about to convince the parents that their son was a worthless tale-teller. The boy could not prove that the Lender had said what he claimed. The parents could not prove the truth of what the boy had told them and the Lender was feeling more and more confident that he would not only have his money back but also the evil pleasure of having tricked the lad.

But one problem persisted. Even if the Lender could convince the parents of their son's untruthfulness, the fact remained that there was no money with which to repay the debt.

When the rich man realized this, he angrily cursed the family and vowed to take the case before the village Mandarin.[9]

Now the kindly Mandarin, as was his procedure in such cases, called in each of the persons involved and listened carefully to all sides of the issue. After he had heard them out, he called in Due, his parents, and the rich man together.

The mandarin turned to the boy and addressed him first. "Tell us, Son, now that this Lender denies any such agreement as you have claimed, was there any witness to the conversation that you say went on between you and this man? Did anyone over hear this man promise you that he would forget the debt owed him by your family if you would explain the riddle of your parents' whereabouts?"

"Yes, there was," Due replied quickly. "Thach Sung, the lizard was balancing himself on the end of my mother's large cooking chopsticks and they were proped against the charcoal stove. He couldn't help but hear everything we said."

Before the Mandarin could continue his questioning, the Lender jumped to his feet.

"Not so!" interrupted the Lender. "The lizard was not on the chopsticks. We both saw him on the ceiling!" he cried.

No sooner had the Lender spoken these words than he realized he had been most cleverly tricked by the young boy.

The Mandarin also noted the boy's clever method of proving his honesty and exposing the Lender.

The Mandarin ruled against the rich man, admonishing him to give up his cunning ways and to live up to his promises.

The wise old Mandarin took an immediate liking to the lad for his quick mind and his honest and forthright manner. So he offered to help him, that one day Due might indeed go beyond the mountains, become a scholar, and learn the answers to those many questions he had while lying, dreaming, on the broad powerful back of his old friend, Trâu Khổng Lồ.

MONSOON

During the reign of the great Hung Vuong 18, Vietnam very nearly came to an end. Great waves "chồm"[10] from the sea and "lướt tới" the land in a "điên" and angry frenzy. They "quất" and lashed the villages then "lôi" them mercilessly into the sea. Rain "rơi" like darts from the heavens until valleys and lowlands became whirling pools. Quiet streams turned into raging rivers. Winds "dụt" and tore at trees and plants and "tung" huge boulders high into the air in "lôi đình."

And how did all this come to be? Why all because of the love of two mighty kings for the same princess.

Now although many noble men had sought the hand of the magnificent beauty, My Nuong, the great Hung Vuong 18 had made it known that his daughter was worthy to marry only the wisest, most powerful ruler on earth.

It so happened that two such rulers lived at that time. Son Tinh was the King of the Mountains. He was strong, just, and calm. His was a peaceful reign for he sought to bring happiness to the land.

The other was Thuy Tinh, King of the Waters. Although Thuy Tinh had a temper of terrible magnitude and was given to sudden, unpredictable storms and would express himself in tidal waves and tornadoes, still there was a softness about him. He would repent his violence and he would offer to take the victims of his rages to the sea bottom where they could dwell in happiness in his kingdom.

Now when Son Tinh and Thuy Tinh heard of Hung Vuong's declaration that only the wisest, most powerful ruler was worthy of his daughter, each decided that he alone was that king.

So they set out for the palace and they both arrived at the same time. Together they petitioned the king for his daughter.

Faced with this dilemma, the Hung Vuong went immediately to council. This was no matter to be taken lightly. Offend either of these kings and who could tell what might happen.

So Hung Vuong and his wise men devised a plan whereby the kings themselves would have to prove which of them was the wisest and most powerful and thus most worthy to marry My Nuong.

"You are both very fine rulers," said Hung Vuong to them. "My daughter is equally drawn to you. Neither she nor I would presume to decide which of you she should marry. That, it is felt, must be decided by yourselves."

"And how may this be done?" asked Son Tinh.

"And what causes you to think that I am possibly not the most powerful," said Thuy Tinh arrogantly.

"Only you can judge each other," continued Hung Vuong. "Certainly with such power as yours must come great wisdom. Therefore, he who first brings to My Nuong fitting wedding gifts is worthy to marry her."

And so it was decided that by the next day each king was to return to the palace with his choice of gifts.

Very early the next morning Son Tinh was at the palace gates.

"Welcome. Welcome." exclaimed Hung Vuong. "We eagerly await you."

With quiet pride, Son Tinh drew from his bag and presented to My Nuong a delicately hand carved ebony box. In it was a single piece of perfect green jade from his mountains far away.

"This," said Son Tinh, "speaks of My Nuong's flawless beauty."

Everyone exclaimed at the gem's perfection. Then he reached into his bag once more. He drew out a piece of purest gold taken from the rocky caverns of his kingdom. He held it before My Nuong and explained, "This gold of finest quality is token of my pure love for you."

Everyone murmured in delight.

Then Son Tinh reached yet another time into his bag. From it he drew a gown made of fabric of such rare delicacy that My Nuong gasped in awe. "This," he said, "is a gift from my mountain folk who spin and weave the country's finest silks. This, My Nuong, is a wedding gown for you."

The princess stood silent before such gifts. Then Son Tinh placed his hand on his chest and said, "This, My Nuong, is my greatest treasure. The gift of my heart."

Everyone stood in reverent respect of the wise Son Tinh for his many gifts that did indeed reveal wisdom, power, and great love.

But according to the agreement, everyone was to wait for Thuy Tinh. Hour followed hour and Thuy Tinh did not appear. Courtiers grew restless and the lovely My Nuong lost interest in the contest so delighted was she with Son Tinh and the lovely presents he had brought.

The sun slipped beyond the far mountains and still Thuy Tinh did not appear.

Thinking that he could not arrive at a decision and fearful that he would have loss of face if he returned in indecision, Hung Vuong decided to give his blessing to Son Tinh and My Nuong. A magnificent ceremony was promptly staged and the two left immediately for their realm in the mountains.

Now it so happened that Thuy Tinh commanded a vast realm. Because of his desire for the lovely My Nuong, he searched his realm over with utmost care for a fitting gift. Finally satisfied with his selection, he set out for the palace. He arrived laden with exquisite pearls and delicate coral in such great quantity that they could not be counted. He brought shells of every description and especially the magic conch shell for within its spirals were contained mighty winds and raging tempests. His final selection was a fine jar in which Thuy Tinh had gathered water from his seas. This he would present to My Nuong as symbol of his entire watery realm which would be hers to rule.

"But Thuy Tinh," explained Hung Vuong, "we believed that you would not return. The day ended and Son Tinh had already came laden with riches. Besides, My Good Man, it would not be possible for My Nuong to live in the sea."

Thuy Tinh could not accept what he heard. His stormy temper began to gather. "If that is the way you would have it then if it is power you wanted to see, you will have your wish. And if you claim that My Nuong could not live in the sea then I'll show you that neither can she live on the land!"

With that Thuy Tinh "thả" lightening and thunder bolts that "rung chuyển" the earth. His winds "gào thét" and hissed and rains "đổ ào ào" against the mountainous realm of Son Tinh.

But the gentle ruler of the land had experienced Thuy Tinh's rage before. No sooner did Thuy Tinh cause the waters to fall than did Son Tinh change it into fog and mist. No sooner did Thuy Tinh attempt to seek out the mountainous kingdom than did Son Tinh take Thuy Tinh's ruinous deluge and turn it into thick clouds that encircled the mountains as refuge for his bride and for his people.

As the waters rose so seemed to rise the mountains. As the rains stripped the slopes they only exposed their core of granite that stood solid against Thuy Tinh's watery tantrum.

At last Thuy Tinh knew he could do no more. In despair he retreated to the sea.

But it was a difficult defeat to accept - to lose one's beloved to another no matter how well he might understand the impossibility of such a love.

And so it is that when the season of monsoon rains comes each year, Vietnamese know that the Ruler of the Sea has not forgotten his lost love. And yet, as Son Tinh cleverly protected his people from Thuy Tinh's destructive rage, so the people of the land know that they are eternally "an toàn" - secure because of the greater power and superior wisdom of the Ruler of the Land.

CRYSTAL LOVE

here lived in the land of languid days and fragrant nights a maiden unequaled by any in her delicate beauty and grace. She lived secluded, hidden away as was the custom, away from the eyes of the young men in the family and village.[11] Hers were the far quarters of the great Mandarin father's palace of ebony and fine teak. Hers were the quiet rooms in which hours and days and weeks of time flowed by as tranquilly as did the silver river flow by her shaded window.

Here did the lovely maiden pass the lonely hours reading, embroidering and dreaming of the man who would come and one day make her his bride.

Often she would gaze from her window at the slow moving river and she would wonder where it had come from and where it was going. She wondered what it had seen along its journey and envied it for what she might never see or know. Sadly, she would turn back to her books and to her dreams.

One evening while she was looking out on the river, she saw a distant fisherman. As his boat moved with the river current, he played a flute. The melody seemed to flow as the river flowed - slowly, pensively, serenely.

Although the fisherman was so far away that the maiden could not see him clearly, still he appeared to be young and strong. She could not make out his face but she imagined it to be fine and handsome.

The Mandarin's daughter was filled with wonder at the plaintive melodies played by the distant fisherman. As she listened, the music seemed to reach out to her as though to take her gently by the hand and lead her from her lonely rooms to all those far off places of her dreams. It seemed to sing of beauty she had not known and of yearnings for which she had no words.

Evening followed evening and the fisherman played his flute as he floated on the far side of the river past the Mandarin's great house. The maiden listened enraptured by what she heard. But there was one melody, one particular refrain which the fisherman played over and over that seemed to call out and caress the lonely girl with its gentle, sad sound.

"Certainly this fisherman is a prince in disguise," she thought. "Surely he passes by each evening, hoping to see me. And his plaintive song must indeed be a song of love, so often does he play it."

Although she knew she must never send for him, nor in anyway show her interest, a day came when she fearlessly prepared to let lotus petals fall softly from her window when she heard his song.

The morning sun rose hot and with it rose her hopes. By her window was the basket of delicate waxen petals.

The late afternoon shadows lengthened. Still the Mandarin's daughter waited.

Deep into the twilight she sat - rigid with anticipation. But finally night fell black and chill and with it fell her expectations.

Nor did the fisherman appear the next evening, nor the next.

Now we know that the life that knows no music is the life that knows not health. And so it was that the lovely young maiden grew ever more pale as her heart grew heavy with sadness.

"You are telling me that my daughter is sick because of love?" the Mandarin frowned at his daughter's servant. "And exactly how could that be?"

The servant unfolded the story of the fisherman and his flute and the Mandarin's heart slowly softened only because of his great love for his daughter.

"If I must, I shall," proclaimed the Mandarin and the fisherman was promptly summoned.

Flanked by servants, the lowly fisherman was escorted through the magnificent doors of the Mandarin's house, down its ornate corridors and to the very bedside of the ailing maiden.

"Look up, My Child," urged the Mandarin. "The longing of your heart is fulfilled. Before you is the maker of the music that once gladdened your heart."

Through her fevered eyes the young girl looked up and into the face of a man more wretched, more ugly than she had ever before seen or imagined. She closed her eyes and she turned her head away in disgust.

The fisherman, however, was awed for the maiden was even more beautiful than any maiden he had ever seen. Yet, seeing her turn her head away so abruptly, he sensed the truth of her feeling.

Quietly, the fisherman was led from the maiden's presence and back to his boat left moored near the great house.

Softly, silently, he played the lovely refrain one final time then floated out of the maiden's life.

Sadness gripped the humble fisherman's shack for he did not return for many days. Finally a search was set. It was found that his lonely boat had drifted far off course and that he had died and drifted with it. Friendly seamen returned the boat with its ill-starred cargo and according to custom, the fisherman's family tenderly cared for his body and then gave it to the earth from which it came. As for the maiden, unaware of the fisherman's sad destiny, she returned to her reading, embroidry and days of dreaming.

Exactly three years passed. In keeping with tradition, the fisherman's family gently removed his body from the earth in order to care for and preserve his bones and thus to free his spirit.

They tenderly lifted the coffin to the earth's surface and prepared for the ritual of cleaning the bones with fragant water, afterwhich they would lay them

47

with reverence in the small, crockery urn that would be their final resting place.[1] [2]

When they opened the coffin they gasped at what they saw. There, gleaming and sparkling in the light of day, lay a piece of flawless crystal.

"How can this be?" they cried. And they stood back because of the brilliance of the stone that lay before them.

"We should find nothing but bones," they exclaimed, "but here we find a perfect heart. Preserved as crystal. A stone of breathless beauty!"

The fisherman's humble family gazed long at the crystal and they pondered this mystery for great had been their love for their crippled brother whose greatest gift to life had been but his lonely, lovely songs.

Years passed and one day the Mandarin's daughter happened to call to her maid servant to bring her tea. Her servant responded with a tray on which sat a porceline tea set and a single fine cup.

"Such a remarkable piece of hand work," exclaimed the Mandarin's daughter as she looked at the fine crystalware. "Where did this come from?"

The servant explained that it was but one of the many gifts given by humble village folk to show honor and respect for her father, the great Mandarin. And she left the room, the tea on the tray beside the crystal cup.

The maiden lifted the pot of tea and poured it into the cup. She set the pot down immediately for suddenly she heard a faint, distantly familiar melody. She looked about the room but saw no one. Then she glanced back at the cup and there to her astonishment, floating on the surface of the tea she saw a tiny boat and in the boat she saw the image of the fisherman.

When she recognized the haunting melody she was overcome with grief for only then did she comprehend that the heart that can make music is more precious than a homely face. She knew then how deeply she had missed the beauty of the fisherman's music. Thus did she guess the fisherman's destiny and what her indifference had accomplished.

The maiden wept tears of remorse and as she did, a tear fell into the cup. When it touched the crystal, the cup shattered into a spray of a million tiny diamonds. Just as quickly they disappeared.

Love, it is believed, is so strong a force that it imprisons the very soul. When one dies of a broken heart, his soul may be forever trapped.

The maiden's tears were tears of contrition and because of them peace was finally brought to the fisherman's soul.[1][3]

And as for the maiden? She resumed her reading and embroidry - but as for her dreams - they were never again so carefree.

TURTLES OF GOLD

AND

BITTER REGRETS

"Ah ha," he said with satisfaction. "This will keep them where they belong!" and the great king, An Duong Vuong, stood back to survey with pride the grand wall his men had constructed to protect his realm from bothersome foreign marauders.

"You are to be congratulated," he nodded approvingly to his Minister of Architecture. You have followed my plan to the finest detail. Such performance merits reward," and the royal inspection party made its way from the site toward the royal compound to celebrate the accomplishment.

But the king stopped mid-track. "And what might this mean?" He directed his question to the Minister of Astrology[14] who was, as always, preoccupied with scrolls and quills, and paper strips. "I say there, isn't this somewhat premature for the onset of the monsoons?"

"Quite so, My good King," blurted the startled astrologer in his attempt to appear alert and also balance his scrolls.

"But according to your current report, your calculations indicated yet a full thirty days before the season of storms."

"Quite right, Sir," and a blurble of muffled explanations came from under the brim of the astrologer's conical cap that had a way of slipping over his face when he jerked his head to abrupt attention.

"I would say, your calculations like your eyes, may have been temporarily obscured," suggested the king. "That sky is filling with clouds and those clouds are being carried on high winds. And those winds are from the sea. That says monsoon to me. What does it say to you, Astrologer?"

"Quite right, Sir...er...I mean, I'm sure there is some very good explanation, My Lord," assured the royal astrologer righting his cap.

51

"Oh, I wouldn't presume to question you there," said the king. "Nor would I question what is happening right now," observed the king. "Run everyone," he commanded and the heavens gave a rollicking laugh and dumped a watery deluge from the sky.

Royal robes were drenched and sagging by the time the party reached shelter. Everyone leaned against the columns of the royal portico, panting for breath.

Suddenly the Minister gave out a lamentable wail "The mortar has had no time to set! The wall can never stand this treatment!"

"But it can and it will, My Good Sir," offered the Minister of Astrology as he jostled limp charts and soggy graphs "My calculations stand. You'll see."

The Minister of Architecture looked at him incredulously then pushed his way to the front of the group to get a better view of the newly completed wall surrounding the northern end of the kingdom.

By this time the heavens were gray on to black. Winds danced and jeered like night witches and rains fell like heavy pages of an ominous tale.

"Do you see what I see?" screamed the Minister of Architecture. "Look there. To the far north end. The wall is moving. It's slipping, I tell you," and the Minister of Architecture turned mournfully away.

Everyone stood horrified.

"This means more than the loss of a wall," bellowed An Duong Vuong. "This means more than wanton waste of time and manpower. You are looking at the loss of protection to our realm! Where is that astrologer?" he growled.

Everyone's head spun this way and that but in the clamor of the thunder and the confusion of the men, the Minister of Astrology like the ink on his soggy, inaccurate charts, had slipped away.

There was no choice.

Nothing could be done but rally tired men and stress already strained muscles. As soon as the rains eased, the wall was again under construction.

"Ah ha," said the king once more as he returned from his second inspection tour. But the party had no sooner turned from the site than the king gasped, "Not again!" Everyone followed the king's eyes heavenward. Clouds were rushing into clear sky like stampeding elephants across serene meadows.

As the royal party ran, rain streaming down their faces and soaking their royal gear, the mighty wall groaned and heaved and toppled once more.

And that very wall fell yet a third time and even a fourth.

At last a council was called. Only the cleverest, the wisest men of the Province were summoned.

"Conspiracy!

Enemies!

Rebels!

Traitors!

Subversives!" they cried.

At long last a very old man with a very long gray beard rose haltingly to his feet, "Will the Son of Heaven be pleased to hear my humble opinion?" he asked.

"Yes, yes. Speak up, old man," urged the king.

"Since the wall was destroyed so many times and always in the same manner," said the old man, "it must be that the gods are against us. Let us try then to appease them by setting up an altar, make sacrifices to them, and ask them to grant us advice and help."

There was a general murmur of approval. The king ordered an altar to be built. Sacrifices were made accordingly. The great king himself fasted for three days and three nights and he prostrated himself in front of the great altar, asking for help.

In time there came a voice, "Son of Heaven, Ruler of the Realm, your prayers are heard."

53

The king rose to his knees, expectant. He looked this way and that. Then he stood to his feet, listening.

"Here I am," came the same voice. "Back here. Behind the altar."

The king stepped to the altar and peered around it. There, standing heavily on four cumbersome legs was a creature of enormous proportions. His great shell rose nearly chest high. Each leg was as thick as three legs of the most powerful of men.

The king blinked his eyes for never had he seen a turtle of such magnitude - nor of such grandeur for this turtle was one of pure gold.

"And who are you, may I ask?" said the king addressing the gold turtle.

"You prayed for help, did you not?" asked the turtle.

"That I did," replied the king.

"And so you have it." asserted the turtle flatly.

"But perhaps you don't understand," continued the king. "My problem is one of great magnitude. It has to do not with animals and ... a ... reptiles but with lives. Many human lives."

"Turtles must never be looked upon lightly," he spoke up somewhat reprimandingly. "Though we may be cumbersome of body, we are usually found to be quite deft of mind."

"I didn't intend disrespect, I assure you," said the king.

"I am sure you didn't since you must know who I really am."

"I confess that I did not know at first, but as you talk on, I become ever more confident of your identity."

"Then you'll be interested in what I have to tell you."

"But indeed," replied the king.

"Then listen with care."

With great patience, the gold turtle explained to the king precisely how the great wall was to be rebuilt. When the king awoke the next morning he set about immediately to follow the turtle's advice.

Ministers stood by in awe as the King took the Master Draftsman's pens directly in hand and began intricate sketches of the proposed wall.

"But my King," gasped the Minister of Architecture, looking on. "My men will have to be master mathematicians to follow such a plan."

"So be it," pronounced the king and he went on furiously sketching and measuring and figuring.

The day arrived when the King was summoned for the inspection.

"Ah ha," declared the king. "This wall will foil any enemy!"

"Indeed it should," muttered the Minister of Architecture to the Minister of Defense. "It has already about foiled both the royal department of building as well as the department of finance. Yet, I am compelled to make one admission. The plan itself is sheer genius. A wall of defense in the shape of a conch shell. Why, until my workmen ran the maze enough to learn it, I nearly lost my entire crew to its twists and turns."

Now although the great wall was finally completed and the kingdom's protection secured, the turtle was to be heard from once more.

"Son of Heaven," he addressed the king in a dream one night. "You now have an impenetratable wall. But you must have one thing more. This country is full of deep rivers and mighty mountains where spirits like to dwell. These spirits are sometimes mischievous and like to play tricks on human beings to show their power.[15] To prevent them from doing so, I offer this to you."

The turtle shifted his weight to three of his legs. He gave his free front leg a powerful shake then gestured to the astonished king to remove his claw.

"When you use my claw as a tumbler of a cross-bow," the turtle went on matter of factly, "it will drive away evil spirits. Moreover, it is capable of destroying a whole army at a single time."

"Now I am quite positive of who you are," said the astounded king in his sleep. "I vow never to question your advice but pledge to follow it willingly always. You know how I care for my people and you have indeed answered my prayer for their safety."

At day break, King An Duong Vuong was awake and issuing orders. First, he commanded that a crossbow be carefully made for the magic claw as its tumbler. Next, he ordered a crystal case fashioned to hold the finished crossbow.

Now at last the mighty king's heart was at rest. He was confident of the protection of the virtuous spirit of the turtle. His people, he knew, could finally enjoy peace and order without fear.

Now the kingdom to the north of An Duong Vuong's realm was under the rule of a powerful emperor. One day, the emperor declared war. He sent a river of men and horses streaming south to invade and to conquer An Duong Vuong's land.

Upon learning of the advancing troops, the king immediately called for the magic crossbow. According to the instructions of the golden turtle, An Duong Vuong raised it and took aim at the approaching army. He pulled back on the heavy cord with all his strength. Then let go. In a blinding fury the crossbow accomplished its amazing feat. The enemy was completely routed before it so much as reached the great spiral wall.

Word of the powerful An Duong spread throughout the land. For several years the people of his kingdom enjoyed peace. Then came fresh warning. The emperor to the north had again sent troops to invade the serene kingdom. This time the enemy took careful precautions. This time the attack came from three directions at once. Soldiers on foot, others by horses, and invaders approached by sea. The An Duong Vuong's kingdom was about to be surrounded.

An Duong Vuong watched calmly from his window as the three mighty units met outside the wall and maneuvered like a menacing swarm of ants around a honey drop. Slowly, cautiously he lifted his miraculous crossbow, took aim, and let the arrow fly. Troops dropped by the hundreds. He took aim again. With the next twang of the great bow, riders and horses fell screaming and neighing. Armor clanged and clamored to the ground. Horses stampeded. What remained of the enemy scurried across the border in utter defeat.

Now the invading general, Trieu Da, although he too retreated, cunningly offered as a gesture of good faith to his victor, his son, Trong Thuy. This he did to suggest his friendship to the victorious An Duong... but he had other motives as well.

"And such a fine young man you are," nodded King An Duong. "I am indeed touched by this gesture of your father. Certainly only one of sincerity and well-meaning would choose to seal his word with his own flesh and blood."

So respectful a young man did the general's son appear to be that in time he gained place for himself in An Duong's court. As a seal of the king's trust, An Duong gave the young man his daughter, My Chau, in marriage.

For a time the young couple knew perfect happiness for the old general's son was indeed taken by the princess and her flawless beauty and charming ways.

And yet, a son, no matter how content his state, never forgets his father nor does he ever completely forget the land of his birth. Day followed day and the young man grew vaguely restless.

Finally the time came when the princess felt she must approach her young husband. "My Lord," she said, "because of my love for you I suffer when I think that you are not as happy as you once were."

"Is it truly love that prompts you to approach me," the young husband asked.

"My Lord, how could you ask that?" replied the princess.

"Because we are from different lands with different ways. There are times when I am not sure."

57

"But you must be sure, My Lord. My love would I willingly prove."

"Then perhaps you might share something of your very own - perhaps some secret that your heart alone holds."

"I would gladly share anything with you. I have nothing to hide. Name it and you will see."

"Why then is it that on certain days you leave our quarters and do not ask that I accompany you nor do you mention where you are going?"

"Why, My Lord, there is no secret to my comings and goings. My respect for you and for our separate ancestory prompts me to do my worshiping alone."

"I see," replied Trong Thuy, but then he continued. "Why is it that at night's blackest the watchman's voice calls out as though it were a distant echo?"

"That is only because of the wall, My Lord."

"The wall?"

"Its shape, My Lord."

"And how might it be shaped that a voice would appear to echo from it?"

"Because of the place the night watchman stands within its spiral walls."

"Spiral walls?"

"Yes, My Lord. Like the magic claw on the holy crossbow, the golden turtle also gave my father the plans for a protective wall which looks ordinary on the outside but whose interior is shaped like a conch shell."

"A conch shell and a crossbow and a golden turtle," mused Trong Thuy. "Tell me," he said aloud, "why have you not talked of these marvelous things before this?"

"But the wall is a subject of common silence and the crossbow is not mine to show," she protested lightly.

"Then perhaps my suspicions have some truth in them."

"Oh do accept my pardon, My Lord, but that is not so," she said and finally, though reluctantly, she expressed her truthfulness and her love by revealing the plans for the great wall. Then she led him to the case of crystal in which lay the magnificent crossbow with the magic claw as its tumbler.

As the young man looked on the magic weapon, a fire ignited within him. Then his eyes caught the lovely princess standing by in her innocence and loyalty and he knew that much of what he felt was tenderness toward her. And yet the claw commanded his gaze for in it he saw a son's respect for an aging father and a whole nation's revenge.

By the dark of the moon, Trong Thuy crept back to the place of the crossbow. Quietly he lifted the lid of the crystal case, reached in, took the magic claw and replaced it with a false one.

After a time, the young man approached the royal household. "I have need to pay my family a visit. Already I have been away from them too long. Please grant me permission to travel to my country."

Although An Duong no longer looked upon Trong Thuy as an enemy, My Chau did not take kindly to his request. "It is a long journey and you must travel through hostile lands. Please reconsider," she begged.

"But it is not right that a son show disrespect to his family by making no attempt to visit them."

"Surely they understand," she pled.

"No father ever truly understands a son who makes no effort to honor him with his presence."[16]

The more the lovely princess beseeched him to stay, the hotter burned the fire within the young husband. Finally he said, "Does this weeping and pleading suit the Most Worshipful Daughter of the great An Duong Vuong? You know that your unworthy servant will come back when I have finished what I must do. Then we shall live together as happily as before."

59

Finally she relented. "There is, of course, no choice but to obey you."

"Your worries are groundless," he persisted. "But if it would ease your heart in my absence, tell me how I would find you if on my return you were not here."

"Does my Lord remember this one thing? Does he recall that it pleased him to give me a coat one time, a coat filled with goose down?"

"I remember well, my Princess," he replied.

"Then hear me out," she said. "If ever a war should occur between our countries while you are away, I will scatter the goose down at the crossroads to show you the way to find me."

Once again Trong Thuy's heart burned within him but this time it was with a searing pain. To both love and to betray was nearly more than the young man could bear.

Yet he bade his love farewell and left hastily for his father's land - not daring to look back.

"Ah ha, my son," smiled the general when Trong Thuy revealed the magic claw to him. "You are all that a father could ever want in a son. Come. Join the celebration, My Boy, for we shall soon rule all lands to the south of us."

"All the lands?" inquired the young man.

"Of course, My Boy. We now have the means to conquer all - and especially the arrogant An Duong Vuong whose court you were wise to leave.

At this, Trong Thuy was stricken with remorse.

Now each night, My Chau prayed alone in her lonely quarters in the palace of An Duong Vuong. She pled with the spirits to return Trong Thuy to her.

Scarcely had the season passed when the watchman approached An Duong Vuong. He flung himself in terror at his feet. "Oh, Great King, Son of Heaven, the enemy is coming once more!"

"Come, come now my good fellow. Let them," said the king, calm at the thought of the power of the magic crossbow. "Have no fear. Return to your post," he comforted him. "No danger will befall this land."

When the watchman had gone, the king called for the crossbow. He lifted it from its crystal case and gazed at it with confidence. Then he strode toward the lookout.

The watchman had been right. The king watched as men poured over the hills and valleys like liquid fire. Horses sped and troops streamed nearer and nearer the great wall.

Calmly, the king positioned the crossbow and set his sight. First to the north, then to the east, then to the south and west he let fly arrows in rapid succession.

But the enemy did not stop.

The king shot the crossbow again and again.

Still the enemy moved forward faster and faster. Over the fields and groves, through the marsh lands and woods they came.

"Saddle my horse," commanded An Duong Vuong in blind bewilderment. With the invaders at the very walls, he swept up My Chau behind him and they fled away to the south.

Past the rice fields. Through the groves. On to the lowlands they sped. Yet as fast as they might ride, so followed the hoof beats behind them.

Past the marshes they went and then to the crossroads.

At last the great sea stretched out before them. In desperation the king lifted his face to the sky and cried out, "Oh, gods, have you forsaken me? And Golden Turtle, why do you not come to my aid?"

But all he could hear was the sound of the waves slapping at the shore before him and the relentless sound of hooves approaching from behind him.

"Oh, Golden Turtle, Virtuous Spirit of the Sea," he cried, "as you have helped me in the past, help me now, I pray thee."

61

From the depths of the sea came a mighty rumble. "Your cry is heard, Son of Heaven, and your plea is answered. Listen with care and beware, I say. Beware of the treacherous one who is behind you."

With that the king reeled about. True to his vow that he would not question the turtle and would forever act on his word, the king drew his sword.

But he saw no one - only the princess standing by shivering like a leaf in a chill wind. Yet in a surge of blind rage and unquestioning obedience he slashed out with fury and pierced the heart of the Princess and her head he let fall into the raging surf.

Stricken instantly with grief at what he had done, An Duong Vuong let the bloody sword fall to the earth and stood, dazed, at the sea's edge. As though responding to the distant spirit's call, the despondent king followed what he perceived to be the voice of the golden turtle and he made his way slowly and forever into the deep.

Faster and faster Trong Thuy urged on his horse, following the goose feather trail. But upon arriving at the scene, his anticipation was dashed like the maddening surf dashes against the rocks then recedes to eternal silence.

Although Trong Thuy saw to a proper burial for his young wife, his soul was never to know peace. Driven by remorse, he met death at the watery depths of a well in the very kingdom he both loved and betrayed.

Legend has it that those oysters who drink of the sea water tinted with the blood of the loyal princess, produce pearls of rare beauty. But should those very pearls be dipped into the water of the well where Trong Thuy drowned himself, their luster would be blinding.

Near the place where the princess, My Chau, died there is a lovely temple. After more than two thousand years, from the time of the ancient Thuc dynasty, people still recall the tragedy of the great king, An Duong Vuong, at the village of Mo Da in north Vietnam.

A STRANGE AND RARE FRIENDSHIP

There is an old Vietnamese saying that if fish is not salted it will spoil and the same for the child who does not obey his parents.

You may be sure that many a hamlet had its share of unsalted fish - those village rascals who chose to disregard their parents' admonitions. Much like those who gave no heed to the equally old saying that as the shirt is made to fit the body below the head, so the child is not wiser than the father.

But now speaking not of unsalted fish but of salted fish and well-fitting shirts, none could be found finer than Luu Binh for he was a young man of such rare privilege that everyone quietly assumed that he would follow worthily in his father's footsteps.

After all, Binh certainly gave the appearance of being all the things a good son should be - handsome and proud in the long black robes of the student. And yet there is a saying that if a child, like a seedling, is not diligently trimmed and trained, when the seedling becomes a tree it will snap in the wind.

Now Binh's father was one of the region's greatest Mandarines. He was dedicated to the well being of each family in his hamlet and he was dedicated to the harmony of the community. But perhaps where young Binh was concerned, assumptions alone were not enough.

As for Binh's life, it was orderly and well directed, or so it seemed to be. It was said that if one were welcomed to the house of Luu Binh and should be so impolite

64

as to miss the appointed time, he would likely find himself directed somewhat stiffly yet cordially to the great guest room, given a polite cup of tea and made to sit for the next most appropriate hour.

But just between you and me, I've a strong idea that if those tardy guests were you and I, we'd not mind altogether. Were you of a curious turn of mind like I find myself to be, you'd have a grand time surrounded by what was so commonplace to Binh yet so dazzling to the likes of us... like watching the way the tropical afternoon sun can splash across a highly polished teak floor and climb like a playful tide up the far walls of the room ... imagining the brocaded cushions of the fine hand carved chairs to be pebbles tumbled smooth and shinning, golden and inviting.

The waves of distant talk and chatter could break over us without our care or comprehending until some servant, efficient because of his careful training, would interrupt our reverie and announce that we could be seen.

And then you'd know, like we all have known at times, the warmth of meeting a very special friend. He would approach you with a smile, hands together and raised to his chin in the formal, cordial greeting used by all Vietnamese.

You'd like his looks, I know. Smooth skin. Hair straight and black. Important looking in his scholar's robes for the young men of this household would, of course, attend the finest schools and have the best tutors.

And possibly, the smallest spark of envy might work its way up within you when you pondered how great would be your pride if you could have been born into such a family. But you'd smother

that spark with a vow to yourself that even though you had not been born to such privilege, still you would somehow succeed. You would somehow find a way to become respected for your knowledge and your wisdom just as everyone expected would be the lot of Luu Binh.

And that's how it might have been for you and me. But as for Duong Le, that's how it was exactly. The orphaned son of a village fisherman and the son of a respected mandarin scholar ... I tell you, such a friendship was virtually unheard of in that country at that time so long ago. Yet, waiting at the servants' door for Le to deliver the Chep (carp) and Thu (cod) that he brought regularly to the great house would be Luu Binh.

Now there is another old saying that if you want wisdom, ask the old but when you want facts, ask the young. So it was that Binh would hold the poor Le with questions of seas and ships and tempests and tides.

"When you finish your deliveries tomorrow, come back," Binh pled. "Come back and tell me more of what it is to live in the village and by the sea."

And so it was that Le's old aunt had given him what advice she could gather as to how to dress and how to behave as a guest at so great a house. "Find out all that you can," Le had urged his aunt, "for it would never do to offend because of ignorance."

But perhaps the distance between life in the great house and life in the fisherman's shack was too much to span in so little a time.

Just how it happened that Le arrived late, I do not know. But when Binh finally came into the grand guest hall to greet Le, awkward formalities soon disappeared.

Now the kindly Mandarin father happened upon the two boys while they were deep in conversation. He was encouraged by what he heard for the good Mandarin had taken note that his son had seemed less and less interested in his studies. It had been a good while since he had seen his son so taken with reciting what he had learned. How good the old Mandarin felt to see the glint of excitement in Binh's eyes as he answered Le's many questions.

Now you and I know that Le's questions had to be very simple for he was but an unschooled fisherman's nephew. But the Mandarin father, inspired by what he overheard, inquired about the young visitor and learned of his lowly background.

"Possibly, just possibly, this is the key I have been looking for," thought the Mandarin.

So he introduced himself to the boy and said to Le, "I see you to be a curious, inquiring lad. I have an idea for you. Come and stay with our family and you may be taught by our tutors.

Le could scarcely believe his ears. He thanked the Mandarin graciously and ran to his old aunt and uncle and told them what had happened. Together they wept for joy for it is said, "Blessed is he whose son is more gifted than he."

Now all the while the tutors had increasing cause for concern and it soon became painfully obvious that there was, living within the walls of the great house, proof of the old proverb that the good that falls through the upper rice sieve can well be caught for use by the tray below - that if good teachings are not utilized by the eldest child, one may find the young making good use of them. For it was not Binh but the fisherman's nephew who was becoming wiser and more learned day by day.

Now the great Mandarin was growing old and his dream of a fine son to take his place was slowly wasting away. Thus it was in great sorrow and bitter disappointment that the old Mandarin finally died. And not long afterwards he was followed by his good wife thus leaving the shiftless Binh with a vast inheritance and meager wisdom.

As the Mandarin's son was now as rich in goods as he was poor in sense, he soon grew haughty and in time took to taunting the fisherman's nephew. But the studious Le would not be dissuaded. He continued his learning with diligence, not forgetting the generosity of his friend's father, the noble Mandarin, nor forgetting what his dear friend, Luu Binh, once was.

Thus it was that Binh was caught in a wheel of days and weeks and months - each following swiftly after the last until his life began to give meaning to the old, old saying that if you sow the wind, you will reap a storm. And in a torrent of spending Binh laid waste the entire family fortune.

With time, the see-saw of life shifted and the young men found themselves firmly in one another's place.

"It isn't right that a friend should suffer so," the once noble Binh complained as he stood, ragged and wasted before Le, the fine young Mandarin. "You have it within your power to help me - to give me money so that I can live as I am accustomed to live. If for no other reason," he persisted, "help me for the sake of the friendship we once knew."

The young Mandarin looked long at the shabby, wretched man and Le was reminded of the wisdom behind the saying that both unsalted fish and untrained children can be good for virtually nothing. And yet, deep was Le's sympathy for Binh and in that moment he knew what the ancients meant when they also said, "Where there is love, ugliness is beauty." Le's heart was heavy because of knowing what Luu Binh could be.

Not allowing his face to betray either his concern or his intent, Le announced to Binh, "According to custom, I will see that you do not go away hungry." He gestured toward the door. "Servants," he called, "conduct this man to the back of the house. Give him morning rice and salted eggplant then send him on his way."

"What is this?" blurted Binh. "Stale rice and bitter vegetable?"

Ignoring his outburst, Le continued, "And Servants, give him two chopsticks - any two chopsticks."

"This cannot be!" cried Binh in disbelief as he looked at the two uneven sticks thrust into his hand.

"It must not be forgotten," continued Le, "that due hospitality is to be shown to each and every beggar that comes to these doors."

"But...but...," stammered Binh.

"Like the uneven chopsticks, a Mandarin need do no more for a wastrel."

"But you...you yourself were once only a..." but the servants led the protesting Binh from the Mandarin's presence.

When he had gone, Le dismissed his servants, closed the doors of his office, and sat alone in sad silence. After a time, the young Mandarin called for Chau Long, the favorite of his young concubines.

"You have been faithful to me," he said. "You have proven your obedience and your love. Only you are worthy of the task I must ask you to perform."

"Take this money," he asserted. "Go and look for a man named Luu Binh. When you find him, tell him that the money will be available to him as he returns to his studies and becomes the respected scholar he was meant to be. Open a tea shop," he went on. "Let it be known that you cater only to scholars. If he wishes to visit you, he must come to the shop. There you will encourage him in his studies."

"But, my Master. This man may be unprincipled. He could pretend to study only to get the money."

"You forget one thing, my lovely Chau Long," Le gently scolded. "You forget that you have it within your power to charge this man with greatness for surely you have not forgotten the saying of your fathers that a man can be rich, thanks to his friends, but he can be noble, thanks only to a woman."

Before Chau Long could protest, Le continued, "You'll do this because of your love for me, as I must do it because of my love for a friend."

Each stood in silence, neither one wanting to be separated from the other.

How true is the wisdom of our people, they pondered, for it has long been said that though a tree may wish to stand still, the wind will never let it.

And so autumn drew out long and warm and one day Luu Binh laughingly said to the beautiful woman in whose shop he enjoyed afternoon tea and relief from his studies, "Can it be that a scholar can have understanding for all else but himself?"

He leaned close to her and whispered, "I lose all hope. I find new life. I lose a friend. I find a love."

"We dare not speak of these things," murmured Chau Long. "There will be time for that. Right now you are so near to being a great Mandarin. You have only to pass your examinations. Nothing must stand in your way."

And so it was that the thread of days rolled round and round and Binh moved steadily toward triumph.

"Chau Long ... Chau Long, where are you?" Binh called one day. "I have news you'll want to hear!"

He burst through the door of the tea shop but was stunned to find that everything seemed suddenly strange to him. Heads nodded toward him in respect. Voices murmured phrases of reverence for the new Mandarin, Luu Binh.

"Tell me, where is Chau Long?" he inquired of a strange young woman standing near.

"Chau Long who?" she replied.

Confused and saddened, Binh asked no more questions but left the tea shop, his elation and dejection as much at odds within him as had been the two

71

uneven chopsticks his friend had given him so long ago.

Without Chau Long to divert him, his mind raced and darted and dove like a kite in a capricious wind and finally settled on the memory of the friend of his youth.

"I wonder how he would feel about me now?" he mused and eventually he set about to find him once more.

Le received Luu Binh graciously and spoke warmly to him of his success.

"Yet there is one thing I would like to know," Binh finally worked the conversation about to ask. He looked steadfastly into the eyes of his old friend as they sat together now as equals. "Why was it that you treated me as you did? Why was it, now so long ago, that you sent me away as you did?"

"You have learned many things, Luu Binh," Le responded, "Yet you have not learned one very important truth."

"Don't misunderstand me, Le. I am able to forgive..."

"Binh," Le interrupted him. "It is not a matter of forgiving. The matter is one of perceiving. But come now, let us speak of other things. Please, have some tea with me." He gestured toward the figure at the end of the room.

As though he were seeing an apparition, Binh stared in shocked silence. There with tray and tea service in hand stood Le's beautiful concubine, Chau Long.

"Can I believe my eyes?" murmured Binh, bewildered. After a time he looked back to his old friend and finally he exclaimed, "Only now do I begin to understand the wisdom of what you did so long ago and the extent of the sacrifice you made for me. Never, I do believe, was there so rare a friendship as this," and he sat, sipping green tea and pondering the ancient Vietnamese saying that there is seldom a teacher so great as one true friend.[17]

THE SISTER QUEENS

n time so long ago that man had only begun to put pen to paper to preserve his country's history, Vietnam was ruled by a mighty kingdom from the North. The Northern Kingdom had seen in its southern neighbor's land many things that it wanted for itself. There were fertile fields, vast irrigated lands, and tidy rice fields that produced magical amounts of shining white kernels. They saw that these people had unlocked the mystery of bronze making and they coveted the gleaming ceremonial figures and vases they saw.

But what the Northern Kingdom had seen that most aroused its lust was a wise and diligent people whose strength and talents it craftily devised to claim as its own.

So it was that the warriors from the north had planned a secret attack. With flashing speed they had descended upon the gentle people and the Southern Kingdom fell without resistance - stunned, crippled and overwhelmed.

The Northern Kingdom ruled the Southern Kingdom with a harsh hand and the people to the south were bent low by the oppression.

One day, Thi Sach, once the Lord of Chau Dien province, secretly called together a small group of the past leaders of the Southern Kingdom. With great caution he laid before them a plan by which he dreamed to overthrow their oppressors. The Lords' hearts burned within them and their desire to free their land kindled their spirits white hot.

But Thi Sach no sooner pledged his followers to the task before them than he was brutally seized and put publically and shamefully to death in the village market place. The northern rulers had cunningly learned of his plot and lost no time in expressing their stand on rebels and traitors.

The villagers mourned the loss of the noble Thi Sach and they mourned the loss of the freedom he sought to restore to them.

With time the people's energies slackened and their wills became crushed. The less they could please their rulers the harsher became the rule. The victors scorned the people and grew arrogant in the confidence that they had successfully enslaved an entire nation.

Now there was at the time a lady by the name of Trung Trac who observed all that was taking place. For a time she hid what she knew. She remained completely composed. She said nothing. Not once did she reveal the deep grief she felt at the loss of her husband, for her husband was the executed Lord, Thi Sach. Not once did she allow her great compassion for her fellow people to be exposed. She kept locked within her all feeling, all thoughts, all plans.

And so it was that one day the Lady held a tea - a quiet, simple, afternoon gathering because spies were most everywhere.

The table was as elegantly set as it could be for a people in bondage and under nearly constant watch. There was the old family porcelain tea service and the delicate fragrance of lotus tea. The room shone with cleanliness. All was properly in its place for the arrival of the ladies of the one-time nobility.

When they arrived they wore the dresses that had once been their loveliest. They brought with them the gossamer-like needlework for which they were so renowned. They seated themselves on the magnificently carved teak couches in the great guest room, took out their sewing, and shared in gentle, guarded tones the latest news of their rulers' intruding ways.

Time passed but the hostess failed to appear. The guests sat sewing long into the afternoon. Tea cups were filled once, twice, and yet a third time. Weary hands began to set down the tedious needlework and questioning glances darted from lady to lady. They shifted their positions and smoothed their dresses and still, they waited.

Suddenly there was a scurry and servants took station at each entry.

Soundlessly, the great doors leading to the next hall began to open. There before the ladies appeared a sight that caused them to gasp and lift kerchiefs to their faces in alarm.

Without the cosmetics that had once added to her great beauty, devoid of the gown of the nobility she once wore with grace and dignity, stood the Lady, Trung Trac. Her robe, her boots, her posture were those of a warrior. In her hand was a sword which she brandished with a skill that caused the ladies to sit in startled silence.

"Sisters, arise!" she commanded.

Her voice was no longer that of a gentlewoman devoted to quiet and domestic calm. Instead, her countenance was one of resolve.

"Listen well to what I say," she continued.

The ladies sat spellbound while Trung Trac laid before them her plan of revenge for the murder of her patriot husband, and her scheme for retaliation against those who held their people for so long against their wills.

Trung Trac's appeal at first shocked her sisters but as they listened their sympathies kindled. In very little time at all the ladies of refinement pledged themselves to Trung Trac and to her vision of freedom.

Within the safety of the dark, at remote places, and secret appointed times, the ladies of the nobility gathered. They tied up their long hair and they belted their flowing dresses and they set themselves to learning the ways of war.

Trung Trac's sister, Trung Nhi, joined with the plan and together the two sisters became mighty leaders. They taught the women swordsmanship until they were every bit as graceful yet as deadly as their male counterparts. They learned to ride and maneuver the lumbering elephant so that he became totally responsive to their gentlest command. They learned strategy and cunning, and finally the time came to strike.

Their attack was as swift as the weaver's singing loom - as direct as the flying shuttle. The enemy Commander at Lien Lau was forced to flee. His

75

troops clambered helplessly after him. Within but a year's time the Trung sisters and their allies held sixty-five citadels.

To shouts of praise and bows of respect and gratitude from the country folk they liberated, the two sisters of the Vietnamese nobility proclaimed themselves, as was their right and place to do, queens of all the lands from the northern to the southern border.

The ceremony took place at Me Linh in the lower Red River Delta. And the villagers once again sang their near-forgotten songs of freedom.

For three years the country people knew peace.[18] Again their rice paddies cradled tender rice shoots in magical abundance. Their market baskets were heaped with freshly picked fruits and laden with vegetables. Fish of every kind lay drying in the sun and hearts were light and free.

But in no way was the kingdom to the north to allow such abundance out of its grasp for long.

The powerful and seasoned General Ma Vien rallied the enemy forces and marched south to the village of Lang Bac. There he dealt the sisters a startling, vengeful blow. The Queens and their forces had no choice but to retreat to the province of Cam Khe and then to the village of Hat Mon. The enemy struck again and again. There, in a decisive battle, the Northern Kingdom once more over powered the gentle kingdom of the south.

But the two heroic queens were not willing to die at the hands of the enemy. They chose rather to go back to the forces of nature which they had so valiantly fought to recover and preserve for their people.

They gave themselves to the gentle waters at that place where the Day and the Red River flow together.

Since that tragic time until now, the courageous Sister Queens, Trung Trac and Trung Nhi, are remembered by two exquisitely beautiful pagodas, one in Hanoi and one in Hat Mon in the province of Son Tay.

Every year on exactly the sixth day of the second month of the lunar year, a day is set aside when all the country of Vietnam honors not only its brave Sister Queens but all the women of their land.

THE LADY OF NAM XUONG

There was, long ago, a great war that raged throughout the country of Vietnam. Faithful countrymen fought long and hard to protect their land from invaders. Though the men of the country knew their territory well and could devise cunning surprise attacks against the enemy, still the power of the invaders continued to threaten the peace of the land.

One such soldier had been but a common farmer known as Truong. His greatest delight in life was to cultivate with care and pride his few fine mangosteen trees that produced a delicious red-rind fruit. Everyone in the village waited for the season when the sun would ripen Truong's mangosteen for beneath its thick peel was a white translucence more pleasing to the tongue than any other sweet.

One day as Truong walked among his mangosteen he heard his name being called. He turned and saw his small son making his way toward him. As he watched this little one, his heart swelled within him. And yet, just as quickly, his thoughts turned gray and heavy like the granite that juts sullenly from the fern covered slopes of the great mountains nearby.

Truong knew that his small, fertile plot of ground and the comfortable though humble home into which he had put such care, were threatened by the enemies to the north.

How could he allow his son to grow up in a country ruled by outsiders? How could he stand by while the very heritage he was to pass on to this child might be ruthlessly seized from him?

As he reached down to gather his first-born into his arms, his heart began to burn within him.

Days went by and the farmer, as was his custom, went about the artful pruning of his fine mangosteen trees so they would not grow too high nor their

branches too numerous. He sculped the trees broad and low so he could be shaded from the summer's harsh sun and so he could reach without difficulty to harvest the fruit. He trimmed with exactness those branches that might rob the tree's juices meant for the main limbs on which were nurtured the delicious fruit.

After that he set about to cultivate and plant a fresh new vegetable garden close to his small house. He tended his rice paddy with special care and saw that all was in order.

And then came the day when he took his wife by the hand and led her to the shade of the finest mangosteen. There, he spoke to her about his decision- the decision he made while going about his work.

"I have no choice," he explained. I must offer myself to the protection of our land. This means that I must leave home and join the others in the fight to save the country."

His wife did not argue with him, nor did she cry or sulk. She was a woman of wisdom and she knew her husband to be a man of decision. She, like her husband, had understood what was happening in their land and she too had known sorrow when she thought of her small son's future.

So the farmer became a fighter and the wife was to learn yet more of wisdom and inner strength.

While the father was away, the little one grew. As he grew, he became ever more curious about his absent father.

Late one April night when the air was thick with heat, and the blackness pressed its heavy way into every corner of their small house, the lonely mother

tried to lull the child to sleep. He was restless and his whimpering would not be stilled. She lit the oil lamp and then took the child in her arms. She rocked him and she sang her sweetest lullabies. Still he would not be quieted.

In desperation, the mother directed the child's attention to the wall beyond his cradle. "Look there, My Child," she said. "I think that is your father now. See there, he is nodding good night to you. He wants you to sleep peacefully and well for you must grow strong."

There, against the lashed bamboo partition seemed to stand a figure, tall and strong, and moving only slightly.

The child looked long at the barely moving form. He seemed comforted and became less and less fitful. The mother laid him in his small bed and his eyelids finally grew heavy with sleep.

When he was quiet, the mother bent down and kissed him. A tear fell lightly on his sleeping face. Then she blew out the lamp and she too gave herself to the night.

Many days passed and the son grew and the youngster faithfully followed as his mother went about the planting and the harvests. Each night, the child slept soundlessly in the knowledge that his father came nightly to bid him well.

Battle raged hot and the farmer-soldier grew skilled in the ways of war. With the same studied manner that he gave himself to his land so he gave himself to the task of preserving that land. Just as he had cultivated with diligence and thus produced mangosteen of finest quality, so his mindfulness to military strategy produced its desired effects. His efforts, as those of his fellowmen, were rewarded. The army dealt the invaders a final crushing blow and sent them whinning in defeat back across the borders of the land.

Then came the day of high celebration and with a victor's stride and a victor's smile, the soldier-farmer turned toward home to reclaim his hard-won little empire.

There in the distance he could see his land. There stood his fine mangosteen. There, his home of sturdy bamboo walls and thick thatched roof. And in the doorway he could see his loving wife, waiting.

As he neared, the father called out to her and the mother in turn cried to the little boy, "The time has come! Your father has returned."

The child came running from his play to stand by his mother and together they waited to greet their soldier-father.

The father ran to them and in his hand he held a silken scarf of finest quality, a gift for his long waiting wife, and with it a tiny toy for his little son. He was about to sweep them both into his arms when unexpectedly the small boy drew back. He stared hard at this man who called himself his father and looked fearfully and questioningly at his mother.

"Come, My Child," encouraged the mother. "Embrace your father. How we have missed him these many, many months!"

But the boy stared at the ground and seemed unable to respond.

"Please, Sir," the boy stammered and drew back. "Please, Sir, I am sorry." Then the boy turned away and said softly, "But you are not my father. My father is very tall and he is very strong."

He held tightly to his mother's skirt and looked uncertainly at the man before him. Then he added, "You cannot be my father because my father comes home to me each night."

The mother stood stunned and speechless and the child clung to her side.

The father looked from the small boy to the boy's mother and back again. A look of comprehension then gathering rage spread across his once jubilant face.

Finally he stabbed the silence with accusation. "This child has been witness to unfaithfulness. How else would he think that some other man is his father?" His fury kindled, the husband grimly added, "You, Wife, have brought dishonor to this family name."[19]

As though mortally wounded by these words and aware of the shame of such a charge, the wife knew that to attempt to argue or dissuade so resolute a man as her husband, would be useless.

At the time when the forest crickets chatter their loudest and when the night winds blow their chillest, the good wife slipped unnoticed from the little home for which she had so tenderly cared in her husband's absence. She ran, blinded by sorrow, to mingle her tears with the waters of the great river that, during the monsoon season, rushes, also blinded, in torrential cascades.

The night was dense and black and the father stirred, restless. He rose to his feet and stumbled about for the oil lamp. The small boy stirred and when the father lit the lamp the child awakened and cried out.

"Look, Sir. Look there." The boy pointed toward the bamboo wall. "There is my father now. He only comes when the work is done and the fire flies blink and the sun has gone to bed. And he's here, like I told you he comes each night."

The father looked where the boy gestured, then he looked at the empty mat near him and he recoiled in horror.

There, because of the way the lamp cast an ever so slightly moving shadow against the bamboo wall, stood what could have passed for the image of a tall, broad-shouldered man.

The little house could not contain the father's grief. He swept his small son into his arms and he ran, calling after his wife.

When he reached the shore of the great river, he stopped, stunned. There in the dim half-light of early dawn lay the silken scarf, caught on a twig at the edge of the rushing water.

He knelt by the edge of the great river and he wept. He pled with the spirits that his wife be told of his terrible error, and that she be freed of his false accusation.

He was given a sign, an assurance, that his plea had already been heard - that heaven had already given honor to this good woman who had died so nobly.

There is, in the village of Nam Xuong, a temple of rare and delicate beauty - a temple that honors the loyalty, obedience and love of a good wife known as the Lady of Nam Xuong.[20]

Nghi ngút đầu ghềnh toả khói hương

Smoke from the burning joss stick
moves slowly through the hills.

Miếu ai như miếu vợ chàng Trương

There, beyond the haze, is that the temple
of the noble wife of Truong?

Ngọn đèn dù tắt đừng nghe trẻ

Had he not believed a child's tale
of shadowy men and dreams,

Sông nước chi cho lụy đến nàng

The great river would not now bear her memory.

Chứng quả có đôi vầng nhật nguyệt

But the sun and moon stand witness.
They knew her faithfulness.

Giải oan chi mượn đến đàn tràng

There was no need for Truong to cry his error.
Her integrity was known
and her soul long since released.

Qua đây mới biết nguồn cơn ấy

Only this day, while passing by this way,
did I learn the tragic tale,

Khá trách chàng Trương quá phũ phàng

And I hereby denounce the brutish Truong
for his unfeeling ways.

King Le Thanh Ton
of Le Dynasty
1442-1497 A.D.

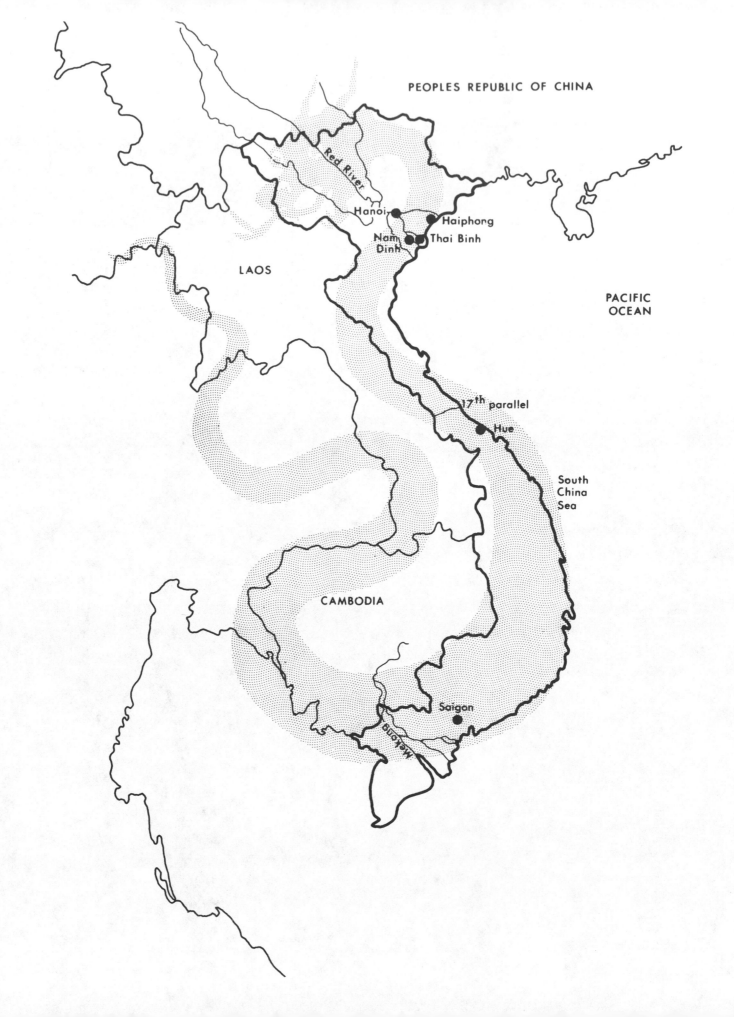

PEOPLES REPUBLIC OF CHINA

Red River

Hanoi

Haiphong

Nam Dinh

Thai Binh

LAOS

PACIFIC OCEAN

17th parallel

Hue

South China Sea

CAMBODIA

Saigon

Mekong

A Very Brief History
of
Vietnam

A distinct Vietnamese people emerged in about the third century B.C. By 208 B.C. much of present-day southern China and northern Vietnam were incorporated into the independent kingdom of Nam Viet.

According to legend, the first born son of the mythical Lac Long Quan, Dragon ruler of the Sea, and his consort, Au Co, Fairy Queen of the mountains, initiated the earliest known Vietnamese ruling family. The Hung (meaning mighty) Vuong (meaning king) dynasty is supposed to have spanned Vietnam's pre-history from 2879 to 259 B.C. or a mythical eighteen generations.

In the legendary tale, "Hung Vuong and the Earth and Sky Cakes," we encounter the dynasty at its seventeenth generation. It is that particular son of Hung Vuong 17 who is least in earthly status but greatest in wisdom who is selected to be Hung Vuong 18 or, so it happens, the last in that dynastic line.

We meet Hung Vuong 18 again in the legend of the "Monsoon." It is his devastatingly beautiful daughter, My Nuong, who because of her desirability sets the forces of nature into conflict. However, Vietnamese legendary history tells us that it is not only Thuy Tinh, the angry king of the waters, who is rejected by My Nuong but there is another rejected suitor as well. Thuc Vuong issues the dying request that his rejection by My Nuong be avenged. It is left to Thuc Phan, his nephew, to accomplish this.

Thus does Thuc Phan set himself against the power of the disintegrating Hung Vuong dynasty and eventually succeeds in wresting the kingdom from Hung Vuong 18. He proclaims himself An Duong Vuong and his rule is reported to have lasted from 257 to 207 B.C.

But as the chain of revenge proceeds unbroken, An Duong Vuong himself meets an untimely end as chronicled in the legend of "Turtles of Gold and Bitter Regrets."

In 111 B.C. Nam Viet was formally annexed to China. Meanwhile, the Indianized state of Funan ruled much of the Mekong Delta area which is present-day South Vietnam.

The North was not freed of Chinese rule until 939 when Ngo Quyen became the first ruler of the new nation of Vietnam. There were, however, periodic attempts to overthrow the oppressive rule of the northerners. One such attempt is told in "The Sister Queens," heroines of the first Vietnamese independence movement around 40 A.D. and a subsequent inspiration to future Vietnamese liberators and freedom fighters.

By 1407, however, Vietnam was reconquered by China. Some ten years later the national hero Le Loi initiated a revolt that cast out the invaders. Under the Le dynasty a Chinese-style bureaucratic government was established and the Vietnamese borders were slowly pushed southward.

By 1750, although the country's southern boundaries were essentially complete, effective central unity had again broken down. The newly established Nguyen dynasty reunified Vietnam by early 1800.

By the late 19th century the country was gradually over-run by the French. Vietnamese rule did not return to the country until Ho Chi Minh's proclamation of an independent government on September 2, 1945. The French resisted independence movements and Ho Chi Minh led guerrilla warfare against them in the first Indochina war which ended in a Vietnamese victory over the French at Dien Bien Phu in May, 1954. The 1954 Geneva Accords provided for a temporary division of the country between a Communist-dominated North and a U.S. supported South.

U.S. intervention and a full-scale war raged from 1965 to 1973. By 1974, however, Northern forces were successful in routing the U.S. presence. Da Nang fell March 29, 1975. By April of that year thousands of Vietnamese refugees were on American soil, having been evacuated from their country by the U.S. government. By May, 1975, Vietnam was a closed country.

NOTES

Were you wondering. . .

1. The legendary account of Lac Long Quan and Au Co was probably not developed in literary form until after A.D. 1200. It is interesting to note that this account shares figures and themes with those found in Chinese mythical history.

   Although very little remains of ancient Chinese creation myths, there is mention of the world-egg concept and some evidence for the notion of a primordial chaos out of which were separated the heaven and earth, the waters and the land.

   The fact that in substance Vietnamese myths contain marked differences from those of China suggests a possible effort by Vietnamese chroniclers to show that in origin and antiquity Vietnam was in no way inferior to the land lying to the north.

2. The lunar calendar is based on the cycles or phases of the moon. By this system each month is normally 30 days in length, with 360 days to a year. When necessary, the extra days are either added to each month or a thirteenth month is created. Whichever method is used, the objective is to keep the calendar year in harmony with the seasonal year.

   To each month, as well as to each year within a twelve-year period, the name of an animal is given.

   There is a whimsical tale about the origin of the lunar system that tells of a kindly diety and his concern for the chaotic condition of time. Thinking how he might right this woeful state, he seized upon a plan. He devised a contest. The participants would be all the animals of the earthly realm over which he presided.

   The conditions of the contest were set. Messengers were dispatched.

   According to the rules, those animals who could make their ways to a pre arranged meeting place would be the winners in the order of their arrival.

   The day of the contest arrived.

   The kindly diety waited.

   Expecting the first arrival to be an animal such as the fleet-footed horse, the diety was surprised when he saw coming into view and ready to claim himself as winner the rat.

   Now the diety knew that some cunning must have gone into the rat's action but he was, by his own rules, bound to honor him.

After a considerable time, there came the lumbering, hard working water buffalo. After the buffalo came the powerful tiger followed by his crony, the cautious cat.

In fifth place came the mighty dragon who was later to become a national symbol of Vietnam. Close behind the dragon slithered the snake.

Everyone stepped back in respect for the friendly yet stately horse who pranced forward, mane and tail flowing gracefully in the soft afternoon air. His place was seventh. Behind him frolicked the goat.

Churbeling merrily, in swung the mischievous monkey followed by the proud, strutting cock.

Next came the faithful dog and last, up waddled the scrupulous pig.

The kindly diety waited until it was evident that no more contestants would arrive. He then declared the contest over.

Now while it was indisputable that the rat made his appearance before the others — even though it was later learned that he had hitched a ride on a cross-countrying elephant — the diety stood by his rules and proclaimed the first year of each twelve-year period as the year of the rat.

But as to the first month of each new year, the diety — given to having the final word, as dieties are prone to have — assigned the tiger who, as all Vietnamese know, is the king of all beasts (lions not being known to Vietnamese jungles, of course.) Thus as each animal was assigned a month, the rat now stood at month eleven.

With a lordly gesture and a heavenly proclamation, time, therefore, took form.

Since that day so many thousands of years ago until this very time, people born in these months are said to have the nature and disposition of their natal animal.

3. The betel nut, in conjunction with the leaf of the betel pepper and a pellet of lime, is used for chewing throughout wide areas of southern Asia. The combination of substances causes salivation and release of stimulating alkaloids. Chewing results in a flow of brick-red saliva which may temporarily dye the mouth orange brown. Contrary to popular belief however, the teeth of habitual chewers are not blackened by betel juice.

4. The Hung Vuong dynasty is thought to have come into existence in 2879 B.C. and to have lasted a mythical eighteen generations or until 259 B.C.

For a better understanding of Vietnamese history from which the legends emerged, see the brief history of the country on page 91.

5. The Vietnamese writing of a proper name places the family name first.

   Due is pronounced Zu — ee

6. Trau means buffalo.

   Khong Lo means large and powerful.

7. The lichee is a fruit which consists of a thin, brittle shell that encloses a sweet, white, jelly-like pulp and a single seed.

8. The longan is a rather spherical, yellowish brown fruit related to the lichee.

9. A mandarin was a scholar and public official who was noted for his knowledge and wisdom in dealing with individual and civic affairs.

10. Vietnamese words have been used because of their lyrically descriptive quality.

chồm	leaped	tung	threw
lướt tới	rushed at	lôi đình	mad frenzy
điên	insane	thả	sent
quất	beat	rung chuyển	trembled
lôi	pulled	gào thét	howled
rơi	fell	đổ ào ào	fell thunderously
dựt	ripped	an toàn	secure

11. In days past, the Vietnamese custom was to assign the unmarried female members of the family to separate quarters. Only did the sexes mingle on special festive occasions. No young woman ventured from her rooms unattended by maid or chaperon.

    Due to the influence of the West, such customs are no longer observed.

12. From earliest times burial rites were an important part of Vietnamese religion and life. It is believed that there exists some sort of continuity of the dead one's personality. Also, there is the belief in the possibility of some contact between the living and the spirit of the dead.

    To many Vietnamese, the community consists of the living, the very personal spirits of dead relatives and intimate friends, and of the less personal spirits of nature — all having the potential of contact with each other. Thus do the place of burial, the manner of burial, and the frequent succeeding commemorations of the dead take on significance in Vietnamese everyday life.

13. It is a commonly held belief among Vietnamese that should a person die while in a state of anxiety — perhaps the result of rejected love, attitudes of hatred, jealousy, or of false accusation — the soul or spirit is not free. Instead, it is caused to hover about in a desperate, ineffectual attempt to communicate with the mortal who was the agent of that anxiety.

    Once that mortal comes into an understanding of his contribution to the plight of the deceased, the realization alone is sufficient to release the spirit to a state of peace.

14. The chief astrologer held a very important place on the royal staff. Because the main industries of the country were agriculture and fishing, the astrologer was responsible for keeping the lunar calendar in order so as to inform the king that he in turn could instruct the people as to the right times for sowing, reaping, and fishing for greatest yield.

15. The belief that natural phenomena such as trees, rocks, rivers, wind and rain contain a spirit or soul is called animism and is a view held by many people of southeast Asia and other parts of the world.

    To worship or revere these spirits is thus a people's endeavor to live harmoniously with the forces of nature.

16. It is held by those influenced by Confucian thought that to be wholly human demands identification with certain codes of behavior which set man apart from the beast.

    One such code requires that the Asian male have three essential allegiances: first, to his king. Next, to his teacher and third, to his father.

    Loyalty to one's king insures national unity. Faith in one's teacher assures perpetuation of accumulated knowledge and wisdom. Reverence for one's father suggests gratitude for the gift of life and also affirms the sanctity and continuence of the family unit.

17. The Asian aphorism or saying is often characterized by a terse comparison between human and natural phenomena, the result of which is a concrete expression of popular wisdom.
    Example:
    What is carved on stone will wear away with time.
    What is taught from mouth to mouth will live forever.

18. Trung Trac and Trung Nhi were heroines of the first Vietnamese independence movement in heading a rebellion against the Chinese Han dynasty overlords and briefly establishing an autonomous state from A.D. 40-43. Their determination and apparently strong leadership qualities are frequently cited by scholars of Southeast Asian culture as testimony to the respected position and freedom of women in Vietnamese society.

19. Because the history of a family is extensive — including many personalities over many generations — the family name gains an identity of its own. Each member therefore wishes to perpetuate the good reputation of the family name for thus will the good name perpetuate each member.

20. The shame associated with the accusation of disloyalty in marriage was, in years past, so great that for the accused to do away with herself was to gain for herself a certain appearance of honor. Suicide alone has never been regarded in Vietnamese morality as an honorable act.